VERSATILE KNIT OR PLUS SIZES

CLASSIC KNITS FOR REAL WOMEN

MARTIN STOREY AND SHARON BRANT

PHOTOGRAPHS BY PETER WILLIAMS

VERSATILE KNITWEAR DESIGNS FOR PLUS SIZES

CLASSIC KNITS FOR REAL WOMEN

MARTIN STOREY AND SHARON BRANT
PHOTOGRAPHS BY PETER WILLIAMS

ROWAN

First published in 2005 by
Rowan Yarns
Green Mill Lane
Holmfirth
West Yorkshire
HD9 2DX

Art direction, styling and design by
Georgina Rhodes and **Richard Proctor**
Editor **Sally Harding**
Pattern writer **Sue Whiting**
Pattern checker **Stella Smith**

British Library Cataloguing in Publication Data
A catalogue record of this book is available
from the British Library

ISBN 1-904485-42-1
Printed in Singapore

CONTENTS

INTRODUCTION

Not all women are 18 years old and a size 10, and very few knitting pattern books give sizes beyond a 16 (which is the average size in Britain!). The purpose of this book is to offer a range of great designs for women of all ages, in sizes 14 upwards.

Women who love to knit, like all women, often lead quite complex lives: working, caring for children in many cases, and, with luck and if not too tired, enjoying a social life as well. With this in mind, the designs in this book are, first and foremost, adaptable. You can dress them up or down. You can wear them aged 20, 40 or 60 plus. You can wear them walking the dog or pushing the buggy, or to the office, or for a night out after the office. The jacket shown on page 20 (above far left) looks great worn casually with the sleeves pushed up in the daytime, but would also dress up for an evening out when worn over the camisole top shown page 21.

We realize that one length or one style does not suit all, so the designs offer a range of hip lengths and neck styles. Some come in alternative versions, such as the top with a round or a V-neck (on pages 59 and 105), so you can choose what suits you best.

We selected three flattering, go-anywhere, colour palettes — one of cool blues, greys and blacks, another of subtle neutrals and naturals, and a third of warmer, richer autumnal shades — in a range of classic Rowan and Jaeger yarns that work across our increasingly confusing seasons! In keeping with our desire to create designs that real people could wear, we photographed the knitwear in this book without using professional models (a testament to the talent of Peter Williams, the photographer). We are indebted to the women (of varying ages and sizes) who took time out of their busy lives to model the clothes for us and also complemented them with clothes from their own wardrobes: so a truly heartfelt thanks to Marian, Jan, Molly, Bluebell, Poppy, Kristy and Sally. You looked great wearing them and, more importantly, you seemed to enjoy the experience!

Martin Storey and Sharon Brant

COOL COLOURS

This clear, spring-like colour palette
goes with many different colours, but
is particularly good teamed with grey,
white, navy and black, and is great for
the summer, too. It is flattering to wear
for most skin tones and hair colours.
Designs in this section include several
great jackets – some dressy, some
casual – and evening sweaters and
tops in a great selection of yarn types
and weights.

Left The Fringe-trim Coat is wonderfully versatile and very flattering. Knitted in a chunky merino wool yarn, it is both soft and really warm. Wear it with jeans for country walks or dress it up for town with dark grey trousers and a camisole. (Instructions on page 24.)

Right Worked in lightweight merino wool, this great Houndstooth Jacket takes its inspiration from Chanel's classic box shape. Its softly harmonizing grey and pale plum checks are worked in the Fair Isle technique. The cabled trim around the collar and cuffs adds a sophisticated finish. (Instructions on page 26.)

Above *The combination of denim yarn with beads is ideal for both dressing up and down. Here, the Bead-trellis Jacket looks great worn casually with jeans, but would work equally* *well for the evening, with a beaded camisole (see page 21) underneath. (Instructions on page 29.)*

Right *Making this long-line Cable Guernsey is a great way to show off your knitting skills! It is knitted in denim yarn and has a flattering high neck. (Instructions on page 32.)*

Right The Scallop-trim Jacket is knitted in an Aran-weight merino yarn, making it the ideal choice for the autumn or for cool spring days. Great as a casual cover up for the country, it also translates effortlessly into a smart jacket for the office. (Instructions on page 36.)

Above (front) The short denim Bead-trellis Scarf takes its theme from the Bead-trellis Jacket (see page 12). Wear it with a smart plain pullover or jacket for maximum effect. (Instructions on page 35.)

Right This Frilled V-Neck Sweater is feminine and flattering. Knitted in a lightweight cotton yarn, it is ideal for summer evenings and smart enough to carry on from the office to an evening out. (Instructions on page 40.)

Left Beaded loops of a mohair-silk yarn create the frothy collar on the Flower-trim Jacket. Worked in a double-knitting merino yarn, the jacket turns into a classic V-neck cardigan if you omit the collar. (Instructions on page 42.)

Right This elegant cotton Lace-sleeve Sweater keeps you cool but covers you up. It works well as daytime wear and for evening, too. (Instructions on page 48.)

Overleaf
Left The Textured Jacket is a variation on the Beaded Jacket shown on page 69. Knitted in extra fine merino yarn, it is the ideal classic jacket for summer and winter alike. (Instructions on page 96.)

Centre The Poodle-collar Jacket (shown also on page 22) is really versatile and can be worn either as a cover-up for evening or casually for relaxing, as here.

Right Knitted in soft lightweight merino yarn, the Beaded Polo-neck Top looks chic on its own for evening or summer days. It also makes the perfect companion for the Beaded Trellis Jacket on page 12. (Instructions on page 38.)

Left Worked in luxuriously soft mohair-mix yarn, the Poodle-collar Jacket is a really flattering style to wear. The loop stitch for the collar is quick to master and fun to knit. (Instructions on page 45.)

Above The Cable-yoke Jacket is a design for all ages and all sizes. It has a wonderful chunky texture in denim yarn, and features split sides and a fringed hem and collar. A guaranteed classic! (Instructions on page 50.)

FRINGE-TRIM COAT

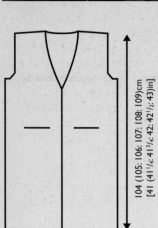

104 (105: 106: 107: 108: 109)cm
[41 (41¼: 41¾: 42: 42½: 43)in]

59.5 (62: 64.5: 67.5: 70: 72.5)cm
[23½ (24½: 25½: 26½: 27½: 28½)in]

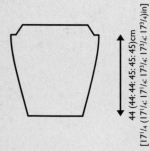

44 (44: 44: 45: 45: 45)cm
[17¼ (17¼: 17¼: 17¾: 17¾: 17¾)in]

SIZES

| 1 | 2 | 3 | 4 | 5 | 6 |

TO FIT BUST

| 91 | 97 | 102 | 107 | 112 | 117 | cm |
| 36 | 38 | 40 | 42 | 44 | 46 | in |

YARN

Jaeger Extra Fine Merino Chunky –
grey and beige tweed (019)

| 31 | 31 | 32 | 33 | 34 | 35 x 50gm |

NEEDLES

1 pair 5mm (no 6) (US 8) needles
1 pair 6mm (no 4) (US 10) needles
5mm (no 6) (US 8) circular needle
2 double-pointed 5mm (no 6) (US 8) needles

TENSION

15 sts and 20 rows to 10cm/4in measured over st st using 6mm (US 10) needles.

BACK

Cast on 89 (93: 97: 101: 105: 109) sts using 5mm (US 8) needles.
Work in garter st for 14 rows, ending with a WS row.
Change to 6mm (US 10) needles.
Beg with a K row, cont in st st until back measures 79 (80: 80: 81: 81: 82)cm/31¼ (31½: 31½: 31¾: 31¾: 32¼)in, ending with a WS row.
Shape armholes
Cast off 3 sts at beg of next 2 rows. 83 (87: 91: 95: 99: 103) sts.
Dec 1 st at each end of next 6 rows. 71 (75: 79: 83: 87: 91) sts.
Cont straight until armhole measures 25 (25: 26: 26: 27: 27)cm/9¾ (9¾: 10¼: 10¼: 10¾: 10¾)in, ending with a WS row.
Shape shoulders and back neck
Cast off 7 (8: 8: 9: 9: 10) sts at beg of next 2 rows. 57 (59: 63: 65: 69: 71) sts.
Next row (RS): Cast off 7 (8: 8: 9: 9: 10) sts, K until there are 12 (11: 13: 13: 14: 14) sts on right needle and turn, leaving rem sts on a holder.

Work each side of neck separately.
Cast off 4 sts at beg of next row.
Cast off rem 8 (7: 9: 9: 10: 10) sts.
With RS facing, rejoin yarn to rem sts, cast off centre 19 (21: 21: 21: 23: 23) sts, K to end.
Complete to match first side, reversing shapings.

POCKET LININGS (make 2)

Cast on 27 sts using 6mm (US 10) needles.
Beg with a K row, work in st st for 36 rows, ending with a WS row.
Break yarn and leave sts on a holder.

LEFT FRONT

Cast on 45 (47: 49: 51: 53: 55) sts using 5mm (US 8) needles.
Work in garter st for 14 rows, ending with a WS row.
Change to 6mm (US 10) needles.
Beg with a K row, cont in st st until left front measures 51 (52: 52: 53: 53: 54)cm/20¼ (20½: 20½: 20¾: 20¾: 21¼)in, ending with a WS row.
Place pocket
Next row (RS): K11, slip next 27 sts onto a holder and, in their place, K across 27 sts of first pocket lining, K to end.
Cont in st st until 10 rows less have been worked than on back to beg of armhole shaping, ending with a WS row.
Shape front slope
Dec 1 st at end of next and foll 0 (2: 1: 1: 2: 2) alt rows, then on every foll 4th row until 42 (43: 46: 48: 49: 51) sts rem.
Work 1 (1: 3: 3: 1: 1) rows, ending with a WS row. (Left front now matches back to beg of armhole shaping.)
Shape armhole
Cast off 3 sts at beg and dec 0 (0: 1: 1: 0: 0) st at end of next row. 39 (40: 42: 44: 46: 48) sts.
Work 1 row.
Dec 1 st at armhole edge of next 6 rows **and at same time** dec 1 st at front slope edge on next (next: 3rd: 3rd: next: next) and foll 4th (4th: 0: 0: 4th: 4th) row. 31 (32: 35: 37: 38: 40) sts.

Dec 1 st at front slope edge **only** on 3rd (3rd: next: next: 3rd: 3rd) and every foll 4th row until 22 (23: 25: 27: 28: 30) sts rem. Cont straight until left front matches back to start of shoulder shaping, ending with a WS row.

Shape shoulder

Cast off 7 (8: 8: 9: 9: 10) sts at beg of next and foll alt row. Work 1 row.

Cast off rem 8 (7: 9: 9: 10: 10) sts.

RIGHT FRONT

Cast on 45 (47: 49: 51: 53: 55) sts using 5mm (US 8) needles.

Work in garter st for 14 rows, ending with a WS row.

Change to 6mm (US 10) needles.

Beg with a K row, cont in st st until right front measures 51 (52: 52: 53: 53: 54)cm/20¼ (20½: 20½: 20¾: 20¾: 21¼)in, ending with a WS row.

Place pocket

Next row (RS): K7 (9: 11: 13: 15: 17), slip next 27 sts onto a holder and, in their place, K across 27 sts of second pocket lining, K to end.

Complete to match left front, reversing shapings.

SLEEVES (both alike)

Cast on 43 (45: 45: 47: 49: 49) sts using 5mm (US 8) needles.

Work in garter st for 20 rows, inc 1 st at each end of 5th and every foll 4th row and ending with a WS row. 51 (53: 53: 55: 57: 57) sts.

Change to 6mm (US 10) needles.

Beg with a K row, cont in st st, inc 1 st at each end of next and every foll 4th (6th: 4th: 6th: 6th: 6th) row to 55 (71: 57: 71: 81: 81) sts, then on every foll 6th (8th: 6th: 8th: -: -) row until there are 75 (75: 77: 77: -: -) sts.

Cont straight until sleeve measures 44 (44: 44: 45: 45: 45)cm/17¼ (17¼: 17¼: 17¾: 17¾: 17¾)in, ending with a WS row.

Shape top

Cast off 3 sts at beg of next 2 rows. 69 (69: 71: 71: 75: 75) sts.

Dec 1 st at each end of next and foll 4 alt rows, then on foll row, ending with a WS row. Cast off rem 57 (57: 59: 59: 63: 63) sts.

MAKING UP

PRESS as described on page 123.

Join both shoulder seams using backstitch, or mattress stitch if preferred.

Front bands and collar

With RS facing and using 5mm (US 8) circular needle, starting and ending at cast-on edges, pick up and knit 119 (120: 120: 122: 122: 124) sts up right front opening edge to start of front slope shaping, 40 (40: 42: 43: 44: 45) sts up right front slope to shoulder, 27 (28: 30: 30: 31: 31) sts from back, 40 (40: 42: 43: 44: 45) sts down left front slope to start of front slope shaping, then 119 (120: 120: 122: 122: 124) sts down left front opening edge. 345 (348: 354: 360: 363: 369) sts.

Row 1 (WS of body, RS of collar): K187 (189: 193: 196: 198: 201), wrap next st (by slipping next st onto right needle, taking yarn to opposite side of work between needles and then slipping same st back onto left needle — when working back across wrapped sts, K tog the st and the wrapped loop), turn.

Row 2: K29 (30: 32: 32: 33: 33), wrap next st and turn.

Row 3: K30 (31: 33: 33: 34: 34), wrap next st and turn.

Row 4: K31 (32: 34: 34: 35: 35), wrap next st and turn.

Row 5: K32 (33: 35: 35: 36: 36), wrap next st and turn.

Row 6: K33 (34: 36: 36: 37: 37), wrap next st and turn.

Cont in this way, working one more st before wrapping next st and turning, until the foll row has been worked:

Row 40: K67 (68: 70: 70: 71: 71), wrap next st and turn.

Row 41: K69 (70: 72: 72: 73: 73), wrap next st and turn.

Row 42: K71 (72: 74: 74: 75: 75), wrap next st and turn.

Row 43: K73 (74: 76: 76: 77: 77), wrap next st and turn.

Row 44: K75 (76: 78: 78: 79: 79), wrap next st and turn.

Cont in this way, working 2 more sts before wrapping next st and turning, until the foll row has been worked:

Next row: K107 (108: 114: 114: 119: 119), wrap next st and turn.

Next row: K to end.

Now cont in garter st across all sts until band measures 5cm/2in from pick-up row, measuring at front opening edges, ending with RS of body facing for next row.

Using 5mm (US 8) double-pointed needles, work fringe cast-off as folls: K3, *(without turning slip these 3 sts to opposite end of needle and bring yarn to opposite end of work pulling it quite tightly across WS of work, K these 3 sts again) 16 times, without turning slip these 3 sts to opposite end of needle and bring yarn to opposite end of work pulling it quite tightly across WS of work, K3tog and fasten off, K next 3 sts of band, rep from * until all sts have been cast off.

Pocket tops (both alike)

Slip 27 sts from pocket holder onto 5mm (US 8) needles and rejoin yarn with RS facing.

Work in garter st for 7 rows.

Cast off knitwise (on WS).

See page 124 for finishing instructions, setting in sleeves using the shallow set-in method.

HOUNDSTOOTH JACKET

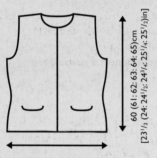

53 (55.5: 58: 60.5: 63: 65.5)cm
[21 (22: 23: 24: 25: 26)in]

60 (61: 62: 63: 64: 65)cm
[23½ (24: 24¾: 24¾: 25¼: 25½)in]

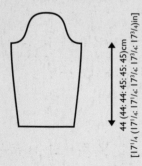

44 (44: 44: 45: 45: 45)cm
[17¼ (17¼: 17¼: 17¾: 17¾: 17¾)in]

SIZES

1	2	3	4	5	6

TO FIT BUST

91	97	102	107	112	117	cm
36	38	40	42	44	46	in

YARNS

Rowan 4 ply Soft
A grey (384)

7	7	8	8	9	9 x 50gm

B light dusty plum (378)

7	7	8	8	9	9 x 50gm

NEEDLES

1 pair 2¾mm (no 12) (US 2) needles
1 pair 3¼mm (no 10) (US 3) needles
Cable needle

BUTTONS – 5

TENSION

32 sts and 29 rows to 10cm/4in measured over
pattern using 3¼mm (US 3) needles.

SPECIAL ABBREVIATIONS

C6B = slip next 3 sts onto cable needle
and leave at back of work, K3, then K3 from
cable needle.

BACK

Cast on 149 (157: 163: 171: 177: 185) sts using
2¾mm (US 2) needles and yarn A.
Row 1 (RS): K1, *P1, K1, rep from * to end.
Row 2: As row 1.
These 2 rows form moss st.
Cont in moss st for a further 11 rows, ending
with a RS row.
Row 14 (WS): Moss st 4 (8: 4: 8: 4: 8) sts,
M1, *moss st 7 sts, M1, rep from * to last 5 (9:
5: 9: 5: 9) sts, moss st to end. 170 (178: 186:
194: 202: 210) sts.
Change to 3¼mm (US 3) needles.
Join in yarn B.
Starting and ending rows as indicated, using the
Fair Isle technique as described on page 123

and repeating the 4 row patt rep throughout,
cont in patt from chart, which is worked
entirely in st st beg with a K row, as folls:
Work 12 rows, ending with a WS row.
Dec 1 st at each end of next and every foll 8th
row until 158 (166: 174: 182: 190: 198) sts rem.
Work 9 rows, ending with a WS row.
Inc 1 st at each end of next and every foll 6th
row until there are 170 (178: 186: 194: 202:
210) sts, taking inc sts into patt.
Cont straight until back measures 37 (38: 38:
39: 39: 40)cm/14½ (15: 15: 15¼: 15½: 15¾)in,
ending with a WS row.
Shape armholes
Keeping patt correct, cast off 6 (7: 7: 8: 8: 9) sts
at beg of next 2 rows. 158 (164: 172: 178: 186:
192) sts.
Dec 1 st at each end of next 9 (9: 11: 11: 13:
13) rows, then on foll 6 (7: 7: 8: 8: 9) alt rows,
then on every foll 4th row until 124 (128: 132:
136: 140: 144) sts rem.
Cont straight until armhole measures 23 (23:
24: 24: 25: 25)cm/9 (9: 9½: 9½: 9¾: 9¾)in,
ending with a WS row.
Shape shoulders and back neck
Cast off 12 (12: 13: 14: 14: 15) sts at beg of next
2 rows. 100 (104: 106: 108: 112: 114) sts.
Next row (RS): Cast off 12 (12: 13: 14: 14:
15) sts, patt until there are 16 (17: 17: 17: 18:
18) sts on right needle and turn, leaving rem sts
on a holder.
Work each side of neck separately.
Cast off 4 sts at beg of next row.
Cast off rem 12 (13: 13: 13: 14: 14) sts.
With RS facing, rejoin yarns to rem sts, cast off
centre 44 (46: 46: 46: 48: 48) sts, patt to end.
Complete to match first side, reversing
shapings.

LEFT FRONT

Cast on 82 (86: 89: 93: 96: 100) sts using 2¾mm
(US 2) needles and yarn A.
Row 1 (RS): *K1, P1, rep from * to last 0 (0:
1: 1: 0: 0) st, K0 (0: 1: 1: 0: 0).
Row 2: K0 (0: 1: 1: 0: 0), *P1, K1, rep from *
to end.

These 2 rows form moss st.
Cont in moss st for a further 11 rows, ending with a RS row.
Row 14 (WS): Moss st 8 sts and slip these sts onto a holder, moss st 2 (4: 2: 4: 2: 4) sts, M1, *moss st 7 sts, M1, rep from * to last 2 (4: 2: 4: 2: 4) sts, moss st to end. 85 (89: 93: 97: 101: 105) sts.
Change to 3¼mm (US 3) needles.
Join in yarn B.
Starting and ending rows as indicated, cont in patt from chart as folls:
Work 12 rows, ending with a WS row.
Dec 1 st at beg of next and every foll 8th row until 79 (83: 87: 91: 95: 99) sts rem.
Work 9 rows, ending with a WS row.
Inc 1 st at beg of next and every foll 6th row until there are 85 (89: 93: 97: 101: 105) sts, taking inc sts into patt.
Cont straight until left front matches back to beg of armhole shaping, ending with a WS row.
Shape armhole
Keeping patt correct, cast off 6 (7: 7: 8: 8: 9) sts at beg of next row. 79 (82: 86: 89: 93: 96) sts.
Work 1 row.
Dec 1 st at armhole edge of next 9 (9: 11: 11: 13: 13) rows, then on foll 6 (7: 7: 8: 8: 9) alt rows, then on every foll 4th row until 62 (64: 66: 68: 70: 72) sts rem.
Cont straight until 15 (15: 15: 15: 15: 17) rows less have been worked than on back to start of shoulder shaping, ending with a RS row.
Shape neck
Keeping patt correct, cast off 8 (9: 9: 9: 10: 9)

sts at beg of next row, then 9 sts at beg of foll alt row. 45 (46: 48: 50: 51: 54) sts.
Dec 1 st at neck edge of next 6 rows, then on foll 3 (3: 3: 3: 3: 4) alt rows, ending with a WS row. 36 (37: 39: 41: 42: 44) sts.
Shape shoulder
Cast off 12 (12: 13: 14: 14: 15) sts at beg of next and foll alt row.
Work 1 row.
Cast off rem 12 (13: 13: 13: 14: 14) sts.

RIGHT FRONT
Cast on 82 (86: 89: 93: 96: 100) sts using 2¾mm (US 2) needles and yarn A.
Row 1 (RS): K0 (0: 1: 1: 0: 0), *P1, K1, rep from * to end.
Row 2: *K1, P1, rep from * to last 0 (0: 1: 1: 0: 0) st, K0 (0: 1: 1: 0: 0).
These 2 rows form moss st.
Cont in moss st for a further 11 rows, ending with a RS row.
Row 14 (WS): Moss st 2 (4: 2: 4: 2: 4) sts, M1, *moss st 7 sts, M1, rep from * to last 10 (12: 10: 12: 10: 12) sts, moss st 2 (4: 2: 4: 2: 4) sts and turn, leaving rem 8 sts on a holder. 85 (89: 93: 97: 101: 105) sts.
Change to 3¼mm (US 3) needles.
Join in yarn B.
Starting and ending rows as indicated, cont in patt from chart as folls:
Work 12 rows, ending with a WS row.
Dec 1 st at end of next and every foll 8th row until 79 (83: 87: 91: 95: 99) sts rem.
Complete to match left front, reversing shapings.

SLEEVES (both alike)
Cast on 78 (80: 80: 82: 84: 84) sts using 3¼mm (US 3) needles and yarn A.
Join in yarn B.
Starting and ending rows as indicated, cont in patt from chart, inc 1 st at each end of 5th and every foll 4th row to 108 (110: 116: 116: 118: 124) sts, then on every foll 6th row until there are 124 (126: 128: 130: 132: 134) sts, taking inc sts into patt.
Cont straight until sleeve measures 42 (42: 42: 43: 43: 43)cm/16½ (16½: 16½: 17: 17: 17)in, ending with a WS row.
Shape top
Keeping patt correct, cast off 6 (7: 7: 8: 8: 9) sts at beg of next 2 rows. 112 (112: 114: 114: 116: 116) sts.
Dec 1 st at each end of next 11 rows, then every foll alt row to 74 sts, then on foll 11 rows, ending with a WS row. 52 sts.
Cast off 5 sts at beg of next 4 rows.
Cast off rem 32 sts.

MAKING UP
PRESS as described on page 123.
Join both shoulder seams using backstitch, or mattress stitch if preferred.
Left front band
Slip 8 sts from left front holder onto 2¾mm (US 2) needles and rejoin yarn A with RS facing.
Cont in moss st as set until band, when slightly stretched, fits up left front opening edge to neck shaping, ending with a WS row.

Key ▪ A ◻ B

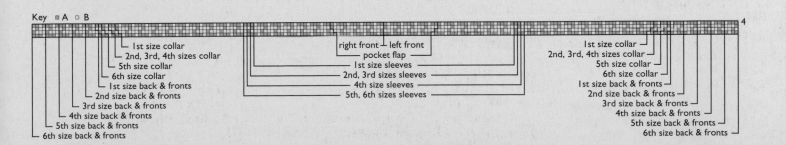

4

1st size collar
2nd, 3rd, 4th sizes collar
5th size collar
6th size collar
1st size back & fronts
2nd size back & fronts
3rd size back & fronts
4th size back & fronts
5th size back & fronts
6th size back & fronts

right front — left front
pocket flap
1st size sleeves
2nd, 3rd sizes sleeves
4th sleeves
5th, 6th sizes sleeves

1st size collar
2nd, 3rd, 4th sizes collar
5th size collar
6th size collar
1st size back & fronts
2nd size back & fronts
3rd size back & fronts
4th size back & fronts
5th size back & fronts
6th size back & fronts

Cast off in moss st.

Slip stitch band in place.

Mark positions for 5 buttons on this band section – first to come 9cm/3½in up from cast-on edge, last to come 1cm/½in below neck shaping, and rem 3 buttons evenly spaced between.

Right front band

Slip 8 sts from right front holder onto 2¾mm (US 2) needles and rejoin yarn A with WS facing.

Cont in moss st as set until band, when slightly stretched, fits up right front opening edge to neck shaping, ending with a WS row and with the addition of 5 buttonholes worked as folls:

Buttonhole row (RS): Moss st 2 sts, work 2 tog, yrn (to make a buttonhole), moss st 4 sts.

Cast off in moss st.

Slip stitch band in place.

Collar

Cast on 156 (160: 160: 160: 164: 168) sts using 3¼mm (US 3) needles and yarn A.

Join in yarn B.

Starting and ending rows as indicated, cont in patt from chart as folls:

Work 1 row, ending with a RS row.

Inc 1 st at each end of next 2 rows, taking inc sts into patt. 160 (164: 164: 164: 168: 172) sts.

Work a further 27 rows, ending with a WS row.

Cast off 20 (21: 21: 21: 21: 22) sts at beg of next 4 rows.

Cast off rem 80 (80: 80: 80: 84: 84) sts.

Pocket flaps (make 2)

Cast on 28 sts using 3¼mm (US 3) needles and yarn A.

Join in yarn B.

Starting and ending rows as indicated, cont in patt from chart as folls:

Work 1 row, ending with a RS row.

Inc 1 st at each end of next 2 rows, taking inc sts into patt. 32 sts.

Work a further 9 rows, ending with a WS row.

Cast off.

Cuff edging (both alike)

Cast on 8 sts using 2¾mm (US 2) needles and yarn A.

Row 1 (RS): P2, K6.

Row 2: P6, K2.

Row 3: P2, C6B.

Row 4: As row 2.

Rows 5 and 6: As rows 1 and 2.

These 6 rows form patt.

Cont in patt until cuff edging fits across cast-on edge of sleeve, ending with a WS row.

Cast off.

Slip stitch un-cabled edge to cast-on edge of sleeve.

Collar edging

Cast on 8 sts using 2¾mm (US 2) needles and yarn A.

Cont in patt as given for cuff edging until collar edging fits around entire row-end and cast-on edges of collar, ending with a WS row.

Cast off.

Slip stitch un-cabled edge in place.

Pocket flap edgings (both alike)

Cast on 8 sts using 2¾mm (US 2) needles and yarn A.

Cont in patt as given for cuff edging until pocket flap edging fits around entire row-end and cast-on edges of pocket flap, ending with a WS row.

Cast off.

Slip stitch un-cabled edge in place.

Sew shaped cast-off edge of collar to neck edge, positioning row-end edge of collar edging halfway across top of front bands.

Using photograph as a guide, sew cast-off edge of pocket flaps to fronts.

See page 124 for finishing instructions, setting in sleeves using the set-in method.

BEAD-TRELLIS JACKET

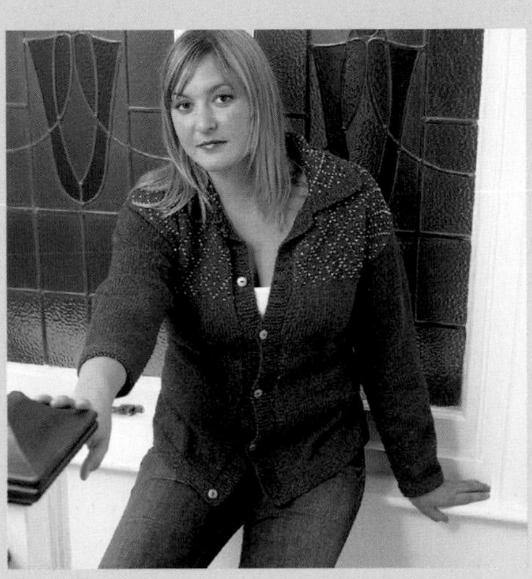

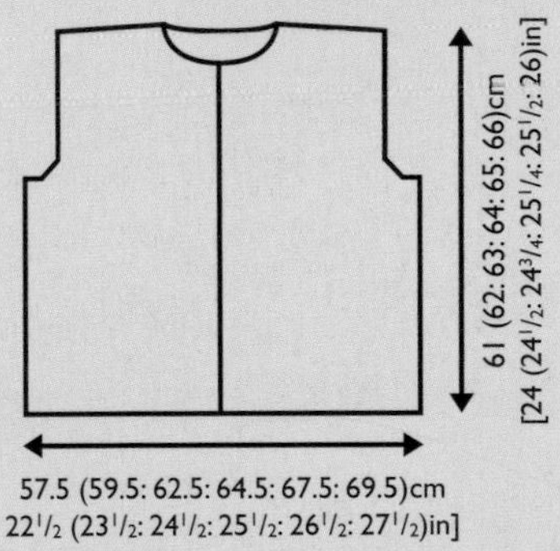
61 (62: 63: 64: 65: 66)cm
[24 (24½: 24¾: 25¼: 25½: 26)in]
57.5 (59.5: 62.5: 64.5: 67.5: 69.5)cm
22½ (23½: 24½: 25½: 26½: 27½)in]

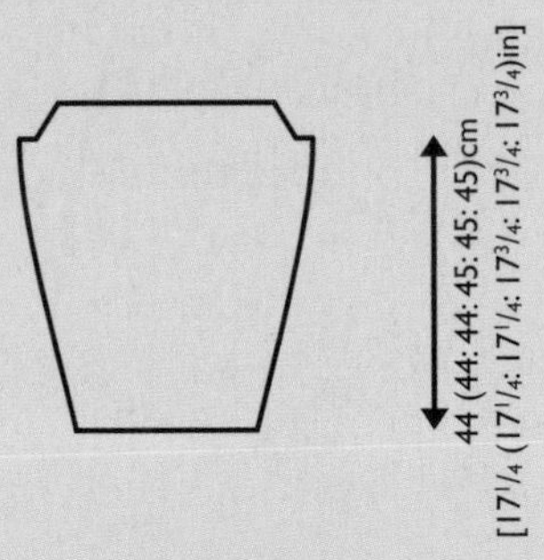
44 (44: 44: 45: 45: 45)cm
[17¼ (17¼: 17¼: 17¾: 17¾: 17¾)in]

SIZES

1	2	3	4	5	6	

TO FIT BUST

91	97	102	107	112	117	cm
36	38	40	42	44	46	in

YARN

Rowan Denim – dark blue (229)

18	19	20	21	22	23 x 50gm

NEEDLES

1 pair 3¼mm (no 10) (US 3) needles
1 pair 4mm (no 8) (US 6) needles

BUTTONS – 6

BEADS – 2,020 (2,130: 2,330: 2,400: 2,660: 2,740) 3mm clear glass beads (Rowan J3000-01008)

TENSION

Before washing: 20 sts and 28 rows to 10cm/4in measured over stocking stitch using 4mm (US 6) needles.

Tension note: Denim will shrink in length when washed for the first time. Allowances have been made in the pattern for shrinkage (see size diagram for after washing measurements).

SPECIAL ABBREVIATION

bead 1 = place a bead by bringing yarn to RS of work and slipping bead up next to st just worked, slip next st purlwise from left needle to right needle and take yarn to WS of work, leaving bead sitting on RS of work in front of slipped st. Do not place beads on edge stitches of work as this will interfere with seaming.

Pattern note: Before starting to knit, thread beads onto yarn. To do this, thread a fine sewing needle (one that will easily pass through the beads) with sewing thread. Knot ends of thread and then pass end of yarn through this loop. Thread a bead onto sewing thread and then gently slide it along and onto knitting yarn. Continue in this way until required number of beads are on yarn.

BACK

Cast on 115 (119: 125: 129: 135: 139) sts using 3¼mm (US 3) needles.
Work in garter st for 12 rows, ending with a WS row.
Change to 4mm (US 6) needles.
Row 13 (RS): Knit.
Row 14: K5, P to last 5 sts, K5.
Rep last 2 rows 10 times more.
Beg with a K row, cont in st st until back measures 44.5 (45.5: 45.5: 46.5: 46.5: 48)cm/17¼ (17¾: 18: 18¼: 18¼: 18¾)in, ending with a WS row.

Shape armholes

Cast off 6 sts at beg of next 2 rows. 103 (107: 113: 117: 123: 127) sts.
Dec 1 st at each end of next and foll 2 alt rows. 97 (101: 107: 111: 117: 121) sts.
Work 1 row, ending with a WS row.
Beg and ending rows as indicated and rep the 16 row patt rep throughout, cont in patt from chart as folls:
Dec 1 st at each end of next and foll 2 alt rows. 91 (95: 101: 105: 111: 115) sts.
Cont straight until armhole measures 27 (27: 28: 28: 29: 29)cm/10¾ (10¾: 11: 11: 11½: 11½)in, ending with a WS row.

Shape shoulders and back neck

Cast off 10 (11: 12: 12: 13: 14) sts at beg of next 2 rows. 71 (73: 77: 81: 85: 87) sts.
Next row (RS): Cast off 10 (11: 12: 12: 13: 14) sts, patt until there are 15 (14: 15: 17: 17: 17) sts on right needle and turn, leaving rem sts on a holder.
Work each side of neck separately.
Cast off 4 sts at beg of next row.
Cast off rem 11 (10: 11: 13: 13: 13) sts.
With RS facing, rejoin yarn to rem sts, cast off centre 21 (23: 23: 23: 25: 25) sts, patt to end.
Complete to match first side, reversing shapings.

LEFT FRONT

Cast on 66 (68: 71: 73: 76: 78) sts using 3¼mm (US 3) needles.

Work in garter st for 11 rows, ending with a RS row.

Row 12 (WS): K8 and slip these sts onto a holder, K to end. 58 (60: 63: 65: 68: 70) sts.

Change to 4mm (US 6) needles.

Row 13 (RS): Knit.

Row 14: P to last 5 sts, K5.

Rep last 2 rows 10 times more.

Beg with a K row, cont in st st until left front matches back to beg of armhole shaping, ending with a WS row.

Shape armhole

Cast off 6 sts at beg of next row. 52 (54: 57: 59: 62: 64) sts.

Work 1 row.

Dec 1 st at armhole edge of next and foll 2 alt rows. 49 (51: 54: 56: 59: 61) sts.

Work 1 row, ending with a WS row.

Beg and ending rows as indicated, cont in patt from chart as folls:

Dec 1 st at armhole edge of next and foll 2 alt rows. 46 (48: 51: 53: 56: 58) sts.

Cont straight until 15 (17: 17: 17: 17: 17) rows less have been worked than on back to start of shoulder shaping, ending with a RS row.

Shape neck

Cast off 7 (7: 7: 7: 8: 8) sts at beg of next row. 39 (41: 44: 46: 48: 50) sts.

Dec 1 st at neck edge of next 4 rows, then on foll 3 (4: 4: 4: 4: 4) alt rows, then on foll 4th row, ending with a WS row. 31 (32: 35: 37: 39: 41) sts.

Shape shoulder

Cast off 10 (11: 12: 12: 13: 14) sts at beg of next and foll alt row.

Work 1 row.

Cast off rem 11 (10: 11: 13: 13: 13) sts.

RIGHT FRONT

Cast on 66 (68: 71: 73: 76: 78) sts using 3¼mm (US 3) needles.

Work in garter st for 4 rows, ending with a WS row.

Row 5 (RS): K3, K2tog, yfwd (to make a buttonhole), K to end.

Work in garter st for a further 6 rows, ending with a RS row.

Row 12 (WS): K to last 8 sts and turn, leaving rem 8 sts on a holder. 58 (60: 63: 65: 68: 70) sts.

Change to 4mm (US 6) needles.

Row 13 (RS): Knit.

Row 14: K5, P to end.

Complete to match left front, reversing shapings.

SLEEVES (both alike)

Cast on 51 (53: 53: 55: 57: 57) sts using 3¼mm (US 3) needles.

Work in garter st for 12 rows, ending with a WS row.

Change to 4mm (US 6) needles.

Beg with a K row, cont in st st, inc 1 st at each end of next and every foll 4th (6th: 4th: 6th: 4th: 4th) row to 55 (89: 63: 97: 65: 65) sts, then on every foll 6th (8th: 6th: -: 6th: 6th) row until there are 93 (93: 97: -: 101: 101) sts.

Cont straight until sleeve measures 51.5 (51.5: 51.5: 52.5: 52.5: 52.5)cm/20¼ (20¼: 20¼: 20¾:

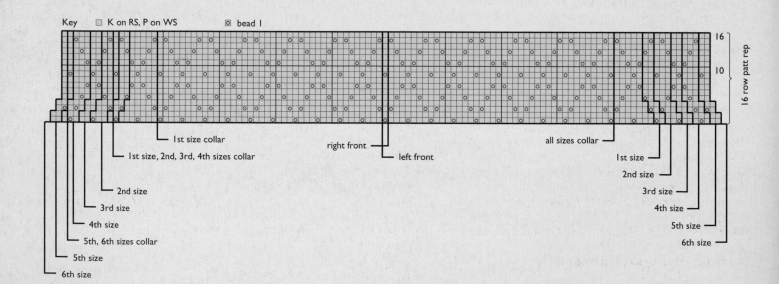

Key   □ K on RS, P on WS   ⊡ bead 1

1st size collar

1st size, 2nd, 3rd, 4th sizes collar

2nd size

3rd size

4th size

5th, 6th sizes collar

5th size

6th size

right front

left front

all sizes collar

1st size

2nd size

3rd size

4th size

5th size

6th size

16

10

16 row patt rep

20¾: 20¾)in, ending with a WS row.
Shape top
Cast off 6 sts at beg of next 2 rows. 81 (81:
85: 85: 89: 89) sts.
Dec 1 st at each end of next and foll 5 alt
rows, then on foll row, ending with a WS row.
Cast off rem 67 (67: 71: 71: 75: 75) sts.

MAKING UP
Do NOT press.
Join both shoulder seams using backstitch, or
mattress stitch if preferred.
Left front band
Slip 8 sts from left front holder onto 3¼mm
(US 3) needles and rejoin yarn with RS facing.
Cont in garter st until band, when slightly
stretched, fits up left front opening edge to
neck shaping, ending with a WS row.
Cast off.
Slip stitch band in place.
Mark positions for 6 buttons on this band
section – first to come level with buttonhole
already worked in right front, last to come
1cm/½in below neck shaping, and rem 4
buttons evenly spaced between.
Right front band
Slip 8 sts from right front holder onto 3¼mm
(US 3) needles and rejoin yarn with WS facing.
Cont in garter st until band, when slightly
stretched, fits up right front opening edge to
neck shaping, ending with a WS row and with
the addition of a further 5 buttonholes
worked as folls:
Buttonhole row (RS): K3, K2tog, yfwd (to
make a buttonhole), K3.
When band is complete, cast off.
Slip stitch band in place.
Collar
Cast on 93 (101: 101: 101: 109: 109) sts using
3¼mm (US 3) needles.
Work in garter st for 6 rows, ending with a
WS row.
Beg and ending rows as indicated, cont in patt
from chart as folls:
Row 7 (RS): K6, work next 81 (89: 89: 89:

97: 97) sts as row 1 of chart, K6.
Row 8: K4, P2, work next 81 (89: 89: 89: 97:
97) sts as row 2 of chart, P2, K4.
These 2 rows set the sts.
Cont as set for a further 30 rows, ending with
a WS row.
Cast off 9 (10: 10: 10: 11: 11) sts at beg of
next 6 rows.
Cast off rem 39 (41: 41: 41: 43: 43) sts.
Machine wash all pieces before completing
sewing together.
Matching ends of collar to centre of bands,
sew cast-off edge of collar to neck edge.
See page 124 for finishing instructions, setting
in sleeves using the shallow set-in method and
leaving side seams open for first 34 rows.

CABLE GUERNSEY

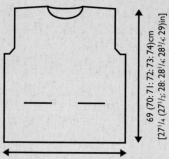

57.5 (59.5: 62.5: 64.5: 67.5: 69.5)cm
[22½ (23½: 24½: 25½: 26½: 27½)in]

69 (70: 71: 72: 73: 74)cm
[27¼ (27½: 28: 28¼: 28¾: 29)in]

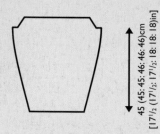

45 (45: 45: 46: 46: 46)cm
[17½ (17½: 17½: 18: 18: 18)in]

SIZES

1	2	3	4	5	6

TO FIT BUST

| 91 | 97 | 102 | 107 | 112 | 117 | cm |
| 36 | 38 | 40 | 42 | 44 | 46 | in |

YARN

Rowan Denim – mid blue (231)

20	21	22	23	24	25 x 50gm

NEEDLES

1 pair 3¼mm (no 10) (US 3) needles
1 pair 4mm (no 8) (US 6) needles
Cable needle

TENSION

Before washing: 20 sts and 28 rows to
10cm/4in measured over st st using 4mm
(US 6) needles.

Tension note: Denim will shrink in length
when washed for the first time. Allowances
have been made in the pattern for shrinkage
(see size diagram for after washing
measurements).

SPECIAL ABBREVIATIONS

C4B = slip next 2 sts onto cable needle and
leave at back of work, K2, then K2 from cable
needle.

C4F = slip next 2 sts onto cable needle and
leave at front of work, K2, then K2 from cable
needle.

C6B = slip next 3 sts onto cable needle and
leave at back of work, K3, then K3 from cable
needle.

C6F = slip next 3 sts onto cable needle and
leave at front of work, K3, then K3 from cable
needle.

BACK

Cast on 115 (119: 125: 129: 135: 139) sts using
3¼mm (US 3) needles.
Row 1 (RS): K1, *P1, K1, rep from * to end.
Row 2: As row 1.

These 2 rows form moss st.
Work in rib for a further 7 rows, ending with a
RS row.
Row 10 (WS): Moss st 10 (12: 15: 17: 20: 22)
sts, M1, (moss st 1 st, M1) twice, moss st 18
sts, M1, (moss st 1 st, M1) twice, moss st 15
sts, M1, (moss st 1 st, M1) twice, moss st 17
sts, M1, (moss st 1 st, M1) twice, moss st 15
sts, M1, (moss st 1 st, M1) twice, moss st 18
sts, M1, (moss st 1 st, M1) twice, moss st to
end. 133 (137: 143: 147: 153: 157) sts.
Change to 4mm (US 6) needles.
Cont in patt, placing chart, as folls:
Row 1 (RS): Moss st 6 sts, K1 (3: 6: 8: 11:
13), work next 119 sts as row 1 of chart for
body, K1 (3: 6: 8: 11: 13), moss st 6 sts.
Row 2: Moss st 6 sts, P1 (3: 6: 8: 11: 13), work
next 119 sts as row 2 of chart for body, P1 (3:
6: 8: 11: 13), moss st 6 sts.
These 2 rows set position of chart.
Keeping sts correct as set, work a further 30
rows, ending with a WS row.**
Now working moss st border sts in ridge patt
(but keeping chart correct), cont straight until
back measures 53.5 (55: 55: 56: 56: 57)cm/21
(21½: 21¾: 22: 22: 22¼)in, ending with a
WS row.
***Shape armholes
Keeping patt correct, cast off 6 sts at beg of
next 2 rows. 121 (125: 131: 135: 141: 145) sts.
Dec 1 st at each end of next and foll 5 alt
rows. 109 (113: 119: 123: 129: 133) sts.
Cont straight until armhole measures 27 (27:
28: 28: 29: 29)cm/10¾ (10¾: 11: 11: 11½:
11½)in, ending with a WS row.
Shape shoulders and back neck
Cast off 12 (12: 13: 14: 14: 15) sts at beg of
next 2 rows. 85 (89: 93: 95: 101: 103) sts.
Next row (RS): Cast off 12 (12: 13: 14: 14:
15) sts, patt until there are 15 (16: 17: 17: 19:
19) sts on right needle and turn, leaving rem
sts on a holder.
Work each side of neck separately.
Cast off 4 sts at beg of next row.
Cast off rem 11 (12: 13: 13: 15: 15) sts.
With RS facing, rejoin yarn to rem sts, cast off

centre 31 (33: 33: 33: 35: 35) sts, patt to end. Complete to match first side, reversing shapings.

POCKET LININGS (make 2)

Cast on 33 sts using 4mm (US 6) needles.
Beg with a K row, work in st st for 51 rows, ending with a RS row.
Row 52 (WS): (P11, M1) twice, P11. 35 sts.
Break yarn and leave sts on a holder.

FRONT

Work as given for back to **, ending with a WS row.
Now working moss st border sts in ridge patt (but keeping chart correct), work 20 rows, ending with a WS row.
Place pockets
Next row (RS): Patt 15 (17: 20: 22: 25: 27)

sts, slip next 35 sts onto a holder and, in their place, patt across 35 sts of first pocket lining, patt 33 sts, slip next 35 sts onto another holder and, in their place, patt across 35 sts of second pocket lining, patt to end.
Work as given for back from *** until 16 (18: 18: 18: 18: 18) rows less have been worked than on back to start of shoulder shaping, ending with a WS row.
Shape neck
Next row (RS): Patt 44 (46: 49: 51: 53: 55) sts and turn, leaving rem sts on a holder.
Work each side of neck separately.
Dec 1 st at neck edge of next 5 rows, then on foll 3 (4: 4: 4: 4: 4) alt rows, then on foll 4th row, ending with a WS row. 35 (36: 39: 41: 43: 45) sts.
Shape shoulder
Cast off 12 (12: 13: 14: 14: 15) sts at beg of

next and foll alt row.
Work 1 row.
Cast off rem 11 (12: 13: 13: 15: 15) sts.
With RS facing, rejoin yarn to rem sts, cast off centre 21 (21: 21: 21: 23: 23) sts, patt to end.
Complete to match first side, reversing shapings.

SLEEVES (both alike)

Cast on 58 (60: 60: 62: 64: 64) sts using 3¼mm (US 3) needles.
Row 1 (RS): K0 (0: 0: 1: 0: 0), P1 (2: 2: 2: 0: 0), (K2, P2) 3 (3: 3: 3: 4: 4) times, *K4, (P2, K2) twice, P2, rep from * twice more, K2, P1 (2: 2: 2: 2: 2), K0 (0: 0: 1: 2: 2).
Row 2 and every foll alt row: P0 (0: 0: 1: 0: 0), K1 (2: 2: 2: 0: 0), (P2, K2) 3 (3: 3: 3: 4: 4) times, *P4, (K2, P2) twice, K2, rep from * twice more, P2, K1 (2: 2: 2: 2: 2), P0 (0: 0: 1: 2: 2).

Sleeve chart

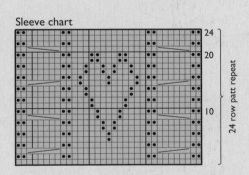

24 row patt repeat

Key

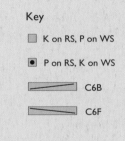

K on RS, P on WS

P on RS, K on WS

C6B

C6F

Body chart

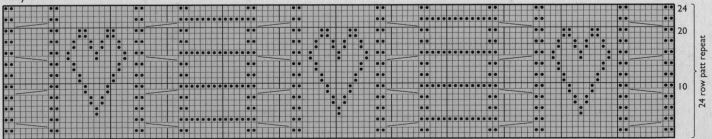

24 row patt repeat

Row 3: K0 (0: 0: 1: 0: 0), P1 (2: 2: 2: 0: 0), (K2, P2) 3 (3: 3: 3: 3: 4: 4) times, *C4B, (P2, K2) twice, P2, rep from * twice more, K2, P1 (2: 2: 2: 2: 2), K0 (0: 0: 1: 2: 2).

Row 5: As row 1.

Row 7: K0 (0: 0: 1: 0: 0), P1 (2: 2: 2: 0: 0), (K2, P2) 3 (3: 3: 3: 3: 4: 4) times, *C4F, (P2, K2) twice, P2, rep from * twice more, K2, P1 (2: 2: 2: 2: 2), K0 (0: 0: 1: 2: 2).

Row 8: As row 2.

These 8 rows form cabled rib patt.

Cont in cabled rib patt for a further 15 rows, ending with a RS row.

Row 24 (WS): Rib 4 (5: 5: 6: 7: 7), (work 2 tog, rib 10) 4 times, work 2 tog, rib to end. 53 (55: 55: 57: 59: 59) sts.

Change to 4mm (US 6) needles.

Cont in patt, placing chart for sleeve, as folls:

Row 1 (RS): K10 (11: 11: 12: 13: 13), work next 33 sts as row 1 of chart for sleeve, K to end.

Row 2: P10 (11: 11: 12: 13: 13), work next 33 sts as row 2 of chart for sleeve, P to end.

These 2 rows set position of chart.

Keeping chart correct, cont as folls:

Rows 3 and 4: K10 (11: 11: 12: 13: 13), work next 33 sts as chart, K to end.

Row 5: Inc in first st, K9 (10: 10: 11: 12: 12), work next 33 sts as chart, K to last st, inc in last st. 55 (57: 57: 59: 61: 61) sts.

Row 6: P11 (12: 12: 13: 14: 14), work next 33 sts as row 6 of chart, P to end.

This 6 rows set the sts – central chart with ridge patt at sides – and start sleeve shaping.

Cont in patt, inc 1 st at each end of 3rd and every foll 4th row to 81 (77: 89: 83: 91: 91) sts, then on every foll 6th row until there are 99 (99: 103: 103: 107: 107) sts, taking inc sts into ridge patt.

Cont straight until sleeve measures 52.5 (52.5: 52.5: 53.5: 53.5: 53.5)cm/20¾ (20¾: 20¾: 21: 21: 21)in, ending with a WS row.

Shape top

Keeping patt correct, cast off 6 sts at beg of next 2 rows. 87 (87: 91: 91: 95: 95) sts.

Dec 1 st at each end of next and foll 5 alt

rows, then on foll row, ending with a WS row. Cast off rem 73 (73: 77: 77: 81: 81) sts.

MAKING UP

Do NOT press.

Join right shoulder seam using backstitch, or mattress stitch if preferred.

Collar

With RS facing and using 3¼mm (US 3) needles, pick up and knit 23 (23: 23: 23: 25: 25) sts down left side of neck, 19 (19: 19: 19: 23: 23) sts from front, 23 (23: 23: 23: 25: 25) sts up right side of neck, then 35 (35: 35: 35: 41: 41) sts from back. 100 (100: 100: 100: 114: 114) sts.

Row 1 and every foll alt row (WS): K2, *(P2, K2) twice, P4, K2, rep from * to end.

Row 2: P2, *C4B, (P2, K2) twice, P2, rep from * to end.

Row 4: P2, *K4, (P2, K2) twice, P2, rep from * to end.

Row 6: P2, *C4F, (P2, K2) twice, P2, rep from * to end.

Row 8: As row 4.

These 8 rows form cabled rib patt.

Cont in cabled rib patt until collar measures 10.5cm/4¼in, ending with a WS row.

Cast off in patt.

Pocket tops (both alike)

Slip 35 sts from pocket holder onto 3¼mm (US 3) needles and rejoin yarn with RS facing.

Row 1 (RS): (K10, K2tog) twice, K11. 33 sts.

Work in moss st as for back for 9 rows.

Cast off in moss st.

Machine wash all pieces before completing sewing together.

See page 124 for finishing instructions, setting in sleeves using the shallow set-in method and leaving side seams open for first 42 rows.

BEAD-TRELLIS SCARF

YARN
Rowan Denim – mid blue (231)
6 x 50gm

NEEDLES
1 pair 3¼mm (no 10) (US 3) needles
1 pair 4mm (no 8) (US 6) needles

BEADS – approx 2,300 3mm clear glass
beads (Rowan J3000-01008)

TENSION
Before washing: 20 sts and 28 rows to
10cm/4in measured over st st using 4mm
(US 6) needles.

Tension note: Denim will shrink in length
when washed for the first time. Allowances
have been made in the pattern for shrinkage.

FINISHED SIZE
Completed scarf measures 20.5cm/8in wide
and 160cm/63in long.

SPECIAL ABBREVIATION
bead 1 = place a bead by bringing yarn to RS
of work and slipping bead up next to st just
worked, slip next st purlwise from left needle
to right needle and take yarn to WS of work,
leaving bead sitting on RS of work in front of
slipped st.

Pattern note: Before starting to knit, thread
beads onto yarn. To do this, thread a fine
sewing needle (one that will easily pass
through the beads) with sewing thread. Knot
ends of thread and then pass end of yarn
through this loop. Thread a bead onto sewing
thread and then gently slide it along and onto
knitting yarn. Continue in this way until
required number of beads are on yarn.

SCARF
Cast on 41 sts using 3¼mm (US 3) needles.
Work in garter st for 4 rows, ending with a
WS row.
Change to 4mm (US 6) needles.
Next row (RS): Knit.
Next row: K3, P to last 3 sts, K3.
Cont in patt as folls:
Row 1 (RS): K4, (bead 1, K3) 9 times, K1.
Row 2 and every foll alt row: K3, P to
last 3 sts, K3.
Row 3: K5, bead 1, (K5, bead 1, K1, bead 1) 3
times, K5, bead 1, K5.
Row 5: K6, (bead 1, K3) 8 times, K3.
Row 7: K7, (bead 1, K1, bead 1, K5) 4 times,
K2.
Row 9: As row 1.
Row 11: As row 7.
Row 13: As row 5.
Row 15: As row 3.
Row 16: As row 2.
These 16 rows form patt.
Rep last 16 rows 31 times more, then rows 1
and 2 again.
Change to 3¼mm (US 3) needles.
Work in garter st for 3 rows.
Cast off knitwise (on WS).

MAKING UP
Machine wash as described on ball band, then
PRESS as described on page 123.

SCALLOP-TRIM JACKET

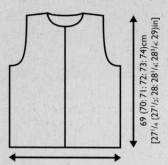

69 (70: 71: 72: 73: 74)cm
[27¼ (27½: 28: 28¼: 28¾: 29)in]

56.5 (58.5: 61.5: 63.5: 67: 69)cm
[22¼ (23: 24¼: 25: 26½: 27¼)in]

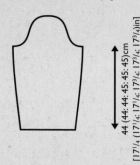

44 (44: 44: 45: 45: 45)cm
[17¼ (17¼: 17¼: 17¾: 17¾: 17¾)in]

SIZES

| 1 | 2 | 3 | 4 | 5 | 6 |

TO FIT BUST

| 91 | 97 | 102 | 107 | 112 | 117 | cm |
| 36 | 38 | 40 | 42 | 44 | 46 | in |

YARNS

Jaeger Extra Fine Merino Aran
A light grey (542)

| 17 | 17 | 18 | 19 | 19 | 20 x 50gm |

Extra Fine Merino DK
B grey tweed (978)

| 1 | 1 | 1 | 1 | 2 | 2 x 50gm |

NEEDLES

1 pair 3mm (no 11) (US 2/3) needles
1 pair 4mm (no 8) (US 6) needles
1 pair 4½mm (no 7) (US 7) needles

BUTTONS – 6

TENSION

19 sts and 25 rows to 10cm/4in measured over st st using 4½mm (US 7) needles and yarn A.

BACK

Cast on 107 (111: 117: 121: 127: 131) sts using 4mm (US 6) needles and yarn A.
Work in garter st for 6 rows, ending with a WS row. Change to 4½mm (US 7) needles.
Next row (RS): Knit.
Next row: K4, P to last 4 sts, K4.
Rep last 2 rows 13 times more, ending with a WS row.
Beg with a K row, cont in st st until back measures 46 (47: 47: 48: 48: 49)cm/18¼ (18½: 18½: 19: 19: 19¼)in, ending with a WS row.
Shape armholes
Cast off 6 (7: 7: 8: 8: 9) sts at beg of next 2 rows. 95 (97: 103: 105: 111: 113) sts.
Next row (RS): K3, K2tog, K to last 5 sts, K2tog tbl, K3.
Next row: P3, P2tog tbl, P to last 5 sts, P2tog, P3.

Working all armhole decreases as set by last 2 rows, dec 1 st at each end of next 1 (1: 3: 3: 5: 5) rows, then on foll 6 alt rows, then on every foll 4th row until 73 (75: 77: 79: 81: 83) sts rem.
Cont straight until armhole measures 23 (23: 24: 24: 25: 25)cm/9 (9: 9½: 9½: 9¾: 9¾)in, ending with a WS row.
Shape shoulders and back neck
Cast off 7 (7: 7: 8: 8: 8) sts at beg of next 2 rows. 59 (61: 63: 63: 65: 67) sts.
Next row (RS): Cast off 7 (7: 7: 8: 8: 8) sts, K until there are 11 (11: 12: 11: 11: 12) sts on right needle and turn, leaving rem sts on a holder. Work each side of neck separately.
Cast off 4 sts at beg of next row.
Cast off rem 7 (7: 8: 7: 7: 8) sts.
With RS facing, rejoin yarn to rem sts, cast off centre 23 (25: 25: 25: 27: 27) sts, K to end.
Complete to match first side, reversing shapings.

LEFT FRONT

Cast on 61 (63: 66: 68: 71: 73) sts using 4mm (US 6) needles and yarn A.
Work in garter st for 5 rows, ending with a RS row.
Next row (WS): K7 and slip these 7 sts onto a holder, K to end. 54 (56: 59: 61: 64: 66) sts.
Change to 4½mm (US 7) needles.
Next row (RS): Knit.
Next row: P2, K1, P4, K1, P to last 4 sts, K4.
Rep last 2 rows 13 times more, ending with a WS row.
Next row (RS): Knit.
Next row: P2, K1, P4, K1, P to end.
Last 2 rows form patt.
Cont in patt until left front matches back to beg of armhole shaping, ending with a WS row.
Shape armhole
Keeping patt correct, cast off 6 (7: 7: 8: 8: 9) sts at beg of next row. 48 (49: 52: 53: 56: 57) sts.
Work 1 row.
Working all armhole decreases as set by back, dec 1 st at armhole edge of next 3 (3: 5: 5: 7: 7) rows, then on foll 6 alt rows, then on every foll 4th row until 37 (38: 39: 40: 41: 42) sts rem.

Cont straight until 13 (13: 13: 13: 13: 15) rows less have been worked than on back to start of shoulder shaping, ending with a RS row.

Shape neck

Cast off 8 (9: 9: 9: 10: 9) sts at beg of next row. 29 (29: 30: 31: 31: 33) sts.

Dec 1 st at neck edge of next 6 rows, then on foll 1 (1: 1: 1: 1: 2) alt rows, then on foll 4th row, ending with a WS row. 21 (21: 22: 23: 23: 24) sts.

Shape shoulder

Cast off 7 (7: 7: 8: 8: 8) sts at beg of next and foll alt row.

Work 1 row.

Cast off rem 7 (7: 8: 7: 7: 8) sts.

RIGHT FRONT

Cast on 61 (63: 66: 68: 71: 73) sts using 4mm (US 6) needles and yarn A.

Work in garter st for 5 rows, ending with a RS row.

Next row (WS): K to last 7 sts and turn, leaving rem 7 sts on a holder. 54 (56: 59: 61: 64: 66) sts.

Change to 4½mm (US 7) needles.

Next row (RS): Knit.

Next row: K4, P to last 8 sts, K1, P4, K1, P2.

Rep last 2 rows 13 times more, ending with a WS row.

Next row (RS): Knit.

Next row: P to last 8 sts, K1, P4, K1, P2.

Last 2 rows form patt.

Complete to match left front, reversing shapings.

SLEEVES (both alike)

Cast on 49 (51: 51: 53: 55: 55) sts using 4½mm (US 7) needles and yarn A.

Beg with a K row, cont in st st, inc 1 st at each end of 5th and every foll 6th row to 55 (57: 65: 65: 67: 75) sts, then on every foll 8th row until there are 73 (75: 77: 79: 81: 83) sts.

Cont straight until sleeve measures 41 (41: 41: 42: 42: 42)cm/16 (16: 16: 16½: 16½: 16½)in, ending with a WS row.

Shape top

Cast off 6 (7: 7: 8: 8: 9) sts at beg of next 2 rows. 61 (61: 63: 63: 65: 65) sts.

Working all decreases as set by back and front armholes, dec 1 st at each end of next 5 rows, then on foll 6 alt rows, then on every foll 4th row until 35 (35: 37: 37: 39: 39) sts rem.

Work 1 row, ending with a WS row.

Dec 1 st at each end of next and every foll alt row to 29 sts, then on foll 5 rows, ending with a WS row.

Cast off rem 19 sts.

MAKING UP

PRESS as described on page 123.

Join both shoulder seams using backstitch, or mattress stitch if preferred.

Left front band

Slip 7 sts from left front holder onto 4mm (US 6) needles and rejoin yarn A with RS facing.

Cont in garter st until band, when slightly stretched, fits up left front opening edge to neck shaping, ending with a WS row.

Break yarn and leave sts on a holder.

Slip stitch band in place.

Mark positions for 6 buttons on this band section – first to come 5cm/2in up from cast-on edge, last to come just above neck shaping, and rem 4 buttons evenly spaced between.

Right front band

Slip 7 sts from right front holder onto 4mm (US 6) needles and rejoin yarn A with WS facing.

Cont in garter st until band, when slightly stretched, fits up right front opening edge to neck shaping, ending with a WS row and with the addition of 5 buttonholes worked as folls:

Buttonhole row (RS): K3, K2tog, yfwd (to make a buttonhole), K2.

When band is complete, do NOT break off yarn.

Slip stitch band in place.

Collar

With RS facing, using 4mm (US 6) needles and yarn A, K 7 from right front band, pick up and knit 22 (23: 23: 23: 25: 25) sts up right side of neck, 31 (33: 33: 33: 35: 35) sts from back, and 22 (23: 23: 23: 25: 25) sts down left side of neck, then K 7 from left front band. 89 (93: 93: 93: 99: 99) sts.

Work in garter st for 3 rows, ending with a WS row.

Next row (RS of body): K3, K2tog, yfwd (to make 6th buttonhole), K to end.

Work in garter st for a further 4 rows.

Cast off 3 sts at beg of next 2 rows. 83 (87: 87: 87: 93: 93) sts.

Cont in garter st until collar measures 12cm/4¾in from pick-up row.

Cast off.

Front trim (make 4)

Cast on 321 (332: 332: 343: 343: 354) sts using 3mm (US 2/3) needles and yarn B.

**Row 1 (WS): Purl.

Row 2: K2, *K1 and slip this st back onto left needle, lift the next 8 sts on left needle over this st and off left needle, (yfwd) twice, K st on left needle again, K2, rep from * to end.

Row 3: K1, *P2tog, (K1, K1 tbl) into double yfwd of previous row, P1, rep from * to last st, K1. 118 (122: 122: 126: 126: 130) sts.

Row 4: Knit.

Cast off knitwise.**

Using photograph as a guide, sew cast-off edge of trims to fronts along P st lines near front bands.

Cuff trims (both alike)

Cast on 145 (145: 145: 156: 156: 156) sts using 3mm (US 2/3) needles and yarn B.

Work as given for front trim from ** to **, noting that there will be 54 (54: 54: 58: 58: 58) sts after row 3.

Sew cast-off edge of trims to cast-on edge of sleeves.

Collar trim

Cast on 343 (354: 354: 354: 376: 376) sts using 3mm (US 2/3) needles and yarn B.

Work as given for front trim from ** to **, noting that there will be 126 (130: 130: 130: 138: 138) sts after row 3.

Sew cast-off edge of trim to outer edge of collar as in photograph.

See page 124 for finishing instructions, setting in sleeves using the set-in method and leaving side seams open for first 34 rows.

BEADED POLO-NECK TOP

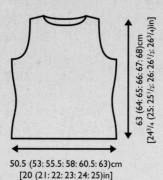

63 (64: 65: 66: 67: 68)cm
[24¾ (25: 25½: 26: 26½: 26¾)in]

50.5 (53: 55.5: 58: 60.5: 63)cm
[20 (21: 22: 23: 24: 25)in]

SIZES

1	2	3	4	5	6

TO FIT BUST

91	97	102	107	112	117	cm
36	38	40	42	44	46	in

YARN

Rowan 4 ply Soft – pale blue (370)

7	7	8	8	8	9 x 50gm

NEEDLES

1 pair 2¾mm (no 12) (US 2) needles
1 pair 3¼mm (no 10) (US 3) needles

BEADS – approx 1,700 (1,800: 1,800: 1,900: 1,900: 2,000) 2.5mm clear glass beads (Rowan J3000-01007)

TENSION

28 sts and 36 rows to 10cm/4in measured over st st using 3¼mm (US 3) needles.

SPECIAL ABBREVIATION

bead 1 = place a bead by bringing yarn to RS of work and slipping bead up next to st just worked, slip next st purlwise from left needle to right needle and take yarn to WS of work, leaving bead sitting on RS of work in front of slipped st. Do not place beads on edge stitches of work as this will interfere with seaming.

Pattern note: Before starting to knit, thread beads onto yarn. To do this, thread a fine sewing needle (one that will easily pass through the beads) with sewing thread. Knot ends of thread and then pass end of yarn through this loop. Thread a bead onto sewing thread and then gently slide it along and onto knitting yarn. Continue in this way until required number of beads are on yarn.

BACK

Cast on 142 (150: 154: 162: 170: 178) sts using 2¾mm (US 2) needles.
Row 1 (RS): K2, *P2, K2, rep from * to end.

Row 2: P2, *K2, P2, rep from * to end.
These 2 rows form rib.
Work in rib for a further 4 rows, dec (dec: inc: inc: dec: dec) 1 st at centre of last row and ending with a WS row. 141 (149: 155: 163: 169: 177) sts.
Change to 3¼mm (US 3) needles.
Beg and ending rows as indicated, working chart rows 1 to 18 once only and then rep rows 19 to 34 throughout, cont in patt from chart as folls:
Work 36 rows, ending with a WS row.
Dec 1 st at each end of next and every foll 10th row to 133 (141: 147: 155: 161: 169) sts, then on every foll 8th row until 129 (137: 143: 151: 157: 165) sts rem.
Work 11 rows, ending with a WS row.
Inc 1 st at each end of next and every foll 8th row until there are 141 (149: 155: 163: 169: 177) sts, taking inc sts into patt.
Cont straight until back measures 42 (43: 43: 44: 44: 45)cm/16½ (16¾: 16¾: 17¼: 17½: 17¾)in, ending with a WS row.

Shape armholes

Keeping patt correct, cast off 7 (8: 8: 9: 9: 10) sts at beg of next 2 rows. 127 (133: 139: 145: 151: 157) sts.
Dec 1 st at each end of next 9 (9: 11: 11: 13: 13) rows, then on foll 7 (8: 8: 9: 9: 10) alt rows, then on foll 4th row. 93 (97: 99: 103: 105: 109) sts.
Cont straight until armhole measures 21 (21: 22: 22: 23: 23)cm/8¼ (8¼: 8¾: 8¾: 9: 9)in, ending with a WS row.

Shape shoulders and back neck

Cast off 6 (7: 7: 8: 8: 8) sts at beg of next 2 rows. 81 (83: 85: 87: 89: 93) sts.
Next row (RS): Cast off 6 (7: 7: 8: 8: 8) sts, patt until there are 11 (10: 11: 11: 11: 13) sts on right needle and turn, leaving rem sts on a holder.
Work each side of neck separately.
Cast off 4 sts at beg of next row.
Cast off rem 7 (6: 7: 7: 7: 9) sts.
With RS facing, rejoin yarn to rem sts, cast off centre 47 (49: 49: 49: 51: 51) sts, patt to end.

Complete to match first side, reversing shapings.

FRONT

Work as given for back until 24 (26: 26: 26: 26: 26) rows less have been worked than on back to start of shoulder shaping, ending with a WS row.

Shape neck

Next row (RS): Patt 32 (34: 35: 37: 37: 39) sts and turn, leaving rem sts on a holder.
Work each side of neck separately.
Dec 1 st at neck edge of next 9 rows, then on foll 1 (2: 2: 2: 2: 2) alt rows, then on every foll 4th row until 19 (20: 21: 23: 23: 25) sts rem, ending with a WS row.

Shape shoulder

Cast off 6 (7: 7: 8: 8: 8) sts at beg of next and foll alt row.
Work 1 row.
Cast off rem 7 (6: 7: 7: 7: 9) sts.
With RS facing, rejoin yarn to rem sts, cast off centre 29 (29: 29: 29: 31: 31) sts, patt to end.
Complete to match first side, reversing shapings.

MAKING UP

PRESS as described on page 123.
Join right shoulder seam using backstitch, or mattress stitch if preferred.

Neckband

With RS facing and using 2¾mm (US 2) needles, pick up and knit 23 (24: 24: 24: 24: 24) sts down left side of neck, 29 (29: 29: 29: 31: 31) sts from front, 23 (24: 24: 24: 24: 24) sts up right side of neck, then 55 (57: 57: 57: 59: 59) sts from back. 130 (134: 134: 134: 138: 138) sts.
Beg with row 1, work in rib as given for back for 7cm/2¾in.
Cast off in rib.
Join left shoulder and neckband seam.

Armhole borders (both alike)

With RS facing and using 2¾mm (US 2) needles, pick up and knit 130 (134: 138: 142: 146: 150) sts all round armhole edge.
Beg with row 1, work in rib as given for back for 5 rows.
Cast off in rib.
See page 124 for finishing instructions.

Key   □ K on RS, P on WS   ⊠ bead 1

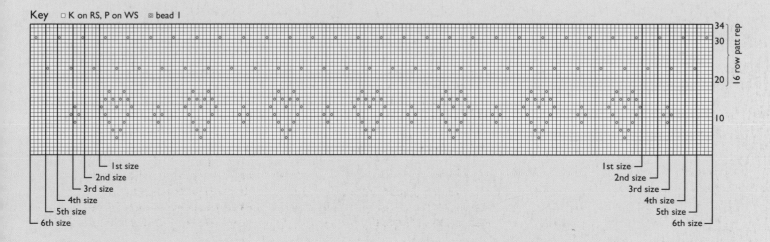

FRILLED V-NECK SWEATER

51 (53: 56: 58: 61: 63)cm
[20 (21: 22: 23: 24: 25)in]

62 (63: 64: 65: 66: 67)cm
[24½ (24¾: 25¼: 25½: 26: 26½)in]

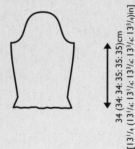

34 (34: 34: 35: 35: 35)cm
[13¼ (13¼: 13¼: 13¾: 13¾: 13¾)in]

SIZES

1	2	3	4	5	6

TO FIT BUST

| 91 | 97 | 102 | 107 | 112 | 117 | cm |
| 36 | 38 | 40 | 42 | 44 | 46 | in |

YARN

Rowan 4 ply Cotton – black (101) or chosen colour

10	10	11	11	12	12 x 50gm

NEEDLES

1 pair 2¼mm (no 13) (US 1) needles
1 pair 3mm (no 11) (US 2/3) needles
2¼mm (no 13) (US 1) circular needle

TENSION

28 sts and 38 rows to 10cm/4in measured over st st using 3mm (US 2/3) needles.

BACK

Cast on 143 (149: 157: 163: 171: 177) sts using 2¼mm (US 1) needles.
Row 1 (RS): K1 (0: 2: 0: 0: 0), P3 (1: 3: 2: 0: 3), *K3, P3, rep from * to last 1 (4: 2: 5: 3: 0) sts, K1 (3: 2: 3: 3: 0), P0 (1: 0: 2: 0: 0).
Row 2: P1 (0: 2: 0: 0: 0), K3 (1: 3: 2: 0: 3), *P3, K3, rep from * to last 1 (4: 2: 5: 3: 0) sts, P1 (3: 2: 3: 3: 0), K0 (1: 0: 2: 0: 0).
These 2 rows form rib.
Cont in rib for a further 6 rows, ending with a WS row.
Change to 3mm (US 2/3) needles.
Beg with a K row, cont in st st, dec 1 st at each end of 29th (33rd: 33rd: 35th: 35th: 37th) and every foll 12th row to 137 (143: 151: 157: 165: 171) sts, then on every foll 10th row to 133 (139: 147: 153: 161: 167) sts, then on foll 8th row. 131 (137: 145: 151: 159: 165) sts.
Work 9 rows, ending with a WS row.
Inc 1 st at each end of next and every foll 8th row until there are 143 (149: 157: 163: 171: 177) sts.
Cont straight until back measures 39 (40: 40: 41: 41: 42)cm/15½ (15¾: 15¾: 16: 16¼: 16¾)in, ending with a WS row.

Shape armholes

Cast off 6 (7: 7: 8: 8: 9) sts at beg of next 2 rows. 131 (135: 143: 147: 155: 159) sts.**
Next row (RS): K3, K2tog, K to last 5 sts, K2tog tbl, K3.
Next row: P3, P2tog tbl, P to last 5 sts, P2tog, P3.
Working all decreases as set by last 2 rows, dec 1 st at each end of next 3 (3: 5: 5: 7: 7) rows, then on foll 4 (5: 5: 6: 6: 7) alt rows, then on every foll 4th row until 109 (111: 115: 117: 121: 123) sts rem.
Cont straight until armhole measures 23 (23: 24: 24: 25: 25)cm/9 (9: 9½: 9½: 9¾: 9¾)in, ending with a WS row.

Shape shoulders and back neck

Cast off 11 (11: 12: 12: 12: 13) sts at beg of next 2 rows. 87 (89: 91: 93: 97: 97) sts.
Next row (RS): Cast off 11 (11: 12: 12: 12: 13) sts, K until there are 15 (15: 15: 16: 17: 16) sts on right needle and turn, leaving rem sts on a holder.
Work each side of neck separately.
Cast off 4 sts at beg of next row.
Cast off rem 11 (11: 11: 12: 13: 12) sts.
With RS facing, rejoin yarn to rem sts, cast off centre 35 (37: 37: 37: 39: 39) sts, K to end.
Complete to match first side, reversing shapings.

FRONT

Work as given for back to **.
Working all armhole decreases as set by back, dec 1 st at each end of next 5 (5: 7: 7: 9: 9) rows, then on foll 4 (5: 5: 5: 4: 4) alt rows, then on foll 4th (0: 0: 0: 0: 0) row. 111 (115: 119: 123: 129: 133) sts.
Work 1 (3: 1: 1: 1: 1) rows, ending with a WS row.

Divide for neck

Next row (RS): (K3, K2tog) 0 (1: 0: 1: 1: 1) times, K55 (52: 59: 56: 59: 61) and turn, leaving rem sts on a holder. 55 (56: 59: 60: 63: 65) sts.
Work each side of neck separately.
Dec 1 st at armhole edge of 2nd (4th: 2nd: 4th: 2nd: 2nd) and foll 0(0: 0: 0: 0: 1) alt row, then

on 0 (0: 1: 1: 2: 2) foll 4th rows **and at same time** dec 1 st at neck edge on 2nd and every foll alt row. 53 (53: 54: 54: 55: 55) sts.
Dec 1 st at neck edge **only** on 2nd and foll 12 (13: 10: 9: 8: 7) alt rows, then on every foll 4th row until 33 (33: 35: 36: 37: 38) sts rem.
Cont straight until front matches back to start of shoulder shaping, ending with a WS row.

Shape shoulder
Cast off 11 (11: 12: 12: 12: 13) sts at beg of next and foll alt row.
Work 1 row.
Cast off rem 11 (11: 11: 12: 13: 12) sts.
With RS facing, rejoin yarn to rem sts, K2tog, K to last 0 (5: 0: 5: 5: 5) sts, (K2tog tbl, K3) 0 (1: 0: 1: 1: 1) times. 55 (56: 59: 60: 63: 65) sts.
Complete to match first side, reversing shapings.

SLEEVES (both alike)
Cast on 63 (65: 65: 67: 69: 69) sts using 3mm (US 2/3) needles.
Beg with a K row, cont in st st, shaping sides by inc 1 st at each end of 5th and every foll 4th row to 67 (69: 81: 79: 87: 93) sts, then on every foll 6th row until there are 95 (97: 101: 103: 107: 109) sts.
Cont straight until sleeve measures 29 (29: 29: 30: 30: 30)cm/11¼ (11¼: 11¼: 11¾: 11¾: 11¾)in, ending with a WS row.

Shape top
Cast off 6 (7: 7: 8: 8: 9) sts at beg of next 2 rows. 83 (83: 87: 87: 91: 91) sts.
Working all decreases as set by armholes, dec 1 st at each end of next 7 rows, then on foll 5 alt rows, then on every foll 4th row until 45 (45: 49: 49: 53: 53) sts rem.
Work 1 row, ending with a WS row.
Dec 1 st at each end of next and every foll alt row to 39 sts, then on foll 5 rows, ending with a WS row.
Cast off rem 29 sts.

MAKING UP
PRESS as described on page 123.
Join both shoulder seams using backstitch.

Neck frill
Cast on 163 (169: 169: 169: 175: 175) sts using 2¼mm (US 1) circular needle.
**Row 1 (WS): K3, *P1, K5, rep from * to last 4 sts, P1, K3.
Row 2: P3, *yon, K1, yfrn, P5, rep from * to last 4 sts, yon, K1, yfrn, P3.
Row 3: K3, *P3, K5, rep from * to last 6 sts, P3, K3.
Row 4: P3, *yon, K3, yfrn, P5, rep from * to last 6 sts, yon, K3, yfrn, P3.
Row 5: K3, *P5, K5, rep from * to last 8 sts, P5, K3.
Row 6: P3, *yon, K5, yfrn, P5, rep from * to last 8 sts, yon, K5, yfrn, P3.
Row 7: K3, *P7, K5, rep from * to last 10 sts, P7, K3.
Row 8: P3, *yon, K7, yfrn, P5, rep from * to last 10 sts, yon, K7, yfrn, P3.
Row 9: K3, *P9, K5, rep from * to last 12 sts, P9, K3.
Row 10: P3, *yon, K9, yfrn, P5, rep from * to last 12 sts, yon, K9, yfrn, P3.
Row 11: K3, *P11, K5, rep from * to last 14 sts, P11, K3.
Row 12: P3, *yon, K11, yfrn, P5, rep from * to last 14 sts, yon, K11, yfrn, P3.
Row 13: K3, *P13, K5, rep from * to last 16 sts, P13, K3.
Row 14: P3, *yon, K13, yfrn, P5, rep from * to last 16 sts, yon, K13, yfrn, P3.
Row 15: K3, *P15, K5, rep from * to last 18 sts, P15, K3.
Row 16: P3, *yon, K15, yfrn, P5, rep from * to last 18 sts, yon, K15, yfrn, P3.
Row 17: K3, *P17, K5, rep from * to last 20 sts, P17, K3.
Row 18: P3, *yon, K17, yfrn, P5, rep from * to last 20 sts, yon, K17, yfrn, P3.
Row 19: K3, *P19, K5, rep from * to last 22 sts, P19, K3.
Row 20: P3, *yon, K19, yfrn, P5, rep from * to last 22 sts, yon, K19, yfrn, P3. 703 (729: 729: 729: 755: 755) sts.
Row 21: K3, *P21, K5, rep from * to last 24 sts, P21, K3.

Work picot cast-off as folls: *cast on 2 sts, cast off 5 sts, slip st on right needle back onto left needle, rep from * until all sts are cast off.**
Join row-end edges of neck frill, then sew cast-on edge to neck edge, positioning seam at centre back neck.

Cuff frills (both alike)
Cast on 67 (67: 73: 73: 73: 73) sts using 2¼mm (US 1) circular needle.
Work as given for neck frill from ** to **, noting that there will be 287 (287: 313: 313: 313: 313) sts after row 20.
Sew cast-on edge of cuff frills to cast-on edge of sleeves.
See page 124 for finishing instructions, setting in sleeves using the set-in method.

FLOWER-TRIM JACKET

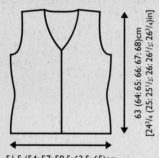

63 (64: 65: 66: 67: 68)cm
[24¾ (25: 25½: 26: 26½: 26¾)in]

51.5 (54: 57: 59.5: 62.5: 65)cm
[20½ (21½: 22½: 23½: 24½: 25½)in]

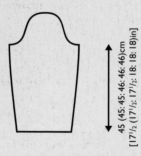

45 (45: 45: 46: 46: 46)cm
[17½ (17½: 17½: 18: 18: 18)in]

SIZES

1	2	3	4	5	6	

TO FIT BUST

91	97	102	107	112	117	cm
36	38	40	42	44	46	in

YARNS

Jaeger Extra Fine Merino DK
A charcoal (959)

13	13	14	15	15	16 x 50gm

Rowan Kidsilk Haze
B dark grey (605)

1	1	1	1	1	1 x 25gm

NEEDLES

1 pair 3mm (no 11) (US 2/3) needles
1 pair 3¾mm (no 9) (US 5) needles

BUTTONS – 6

BEADS – approx 420 2.5mm metallic grey beads (Rowan J3000-01006)

TENSION

22 sts and 30 rows to 10cm/4in measured over st st using 3¾mm (US 5) needles and yarn A.

SPECIAL ABBREVIATIONS

make loop = Insert right needle into next st and take yarn around right needle point as though to K this st, wrap yarn around one finger of left hand then over right needle point again (2 loops on right needle point), draw both these loops through st on left needle slipping st off left needle, insert left needle point into front of both these loops now on right needle and K them tog tbl.
make beaded loop = Insert right needle into next st and take yarn around right needle point as though to K this st, slide bead along yarn leaving it approx 2cm/¾in from right needle point, wrap yarn around one finger of left hand then over right needle point again (2 loops on right needle point) ensuring bead is

on this loop, draw both these loops through st on left needle slipping st off left needle, insert left needle point into front of both these loops now on right needle and K them tog tbl.

BACK

Cast on 113 (119: 125: 131: 137: 143) sts using 3mm (US 2/3) needles and yarn A.
Row 1 (RS): K1, *P1, K1, rep from * to end.
Row 2: As row 1.
These 2 rows form moss st.
Work in moss st for a further 8 rows, ending with a WS row.
Change to 3¾mm (US 5) needles.
Beg with a K row, cont in st st, dec 1 st at each end of 27th (29th: 29th: 29th: 29th: 29th) and every foll 10th row to 107 (113: 119: 125: 131: 137) sts, then on every foll 8th row until there are 103 (109: 115: 121: 127: 133) sts.
Work 7 rows, ending with a WS row.
Inc 1 st at each end of next and every foll 8th row until there are 113 (119: 125: 131: 137: 143) sts.
Cont straight until back measures 40 (41: 41: 42: 42: 43)cm/15¾ (16: 16: 16½: 16¾: 17)in, ending with a WS row.
Shape armholes
Cast off 5 (6: 6: 7: 7: 8) sts at beg of next 2 rows. 103 (107: 113: 117: 123: 127) sts.
Next row (RS): K3, K2tog, K to last 5 sts, K2tog tbl, K3.
Next row: P3, P2tog tbl, P to last 5 sts, P2tog, P3.
Working all armhole decreases as set by last 2 rows, dec 1 st at each end of next 1 (1: 3: 3: 5: 5) rows, then on foll 3 (4: 4: 5: 5: 6) alt rows, then on every foll 4th row until 87 (89: 91: 93: 95: 97) sts rem.
Cont straight until armhole measures 23 (23: 24: 24: 25: 25)cm/9 (9: 9½: 9½: 9¾: 9¾)in, ending with a WS row.
Shape shoulders and back neck
Cast off 9 (9: 9: 9: 9: 10) sts at beg of next 2 rows. 69 (71: 73: 75: 77: 77) sts.
Next row (RS): Cast off 9 (9: 9: 9: 9: 10) sts, K until there are 12 (12: 13: 14: 14: 13) sts on

right needle and turn, leaving rem sts on a holder.

Work each side of neck separately.

Cast off 4 sts at beg of next row.

Cast off rem 8 (8: 9: 10: 10: 9) sts.

With RS facing, rejoin yarn to rem sts, cast off centre 27 (29: 29: 29: 31: 31) sts, K to end.

Complete to match first side, reversing shapings.

LEFT FRONT

Cast on 63 (67: 69: 73: 75: 79) sts using 3mm (US 2/3) needles and yarn A.

Work in moss st as given for back for 9 rows, ending with a RS row.

Row 10 (WS): Moss st 7 sts and slip these onto a holder, moss st to last 1 (0: 1: 0: 1: 0) st, (inc in last st) 1 (0: 1: 0: 1: 0) times. 57 (60: 63: 66: 69: 72) sts.

Change to 3¾mm (US 5) needles.

Beg with a K row, cont in st st, dec 1 st at beg of 27th (29th: 29th: 29th: 29th: 29th) and every foll 10th row to 54 (57: 60: 63: 66: 69) sts, then on every foll 8th row until there are 52 (55: 58: 61: 64: 67) sts.

Work 7 rows, ending with a WS row.

Inc 1 st at beg of next and every foll 8th row until there are 57 (60: 63: 66: 69: 72) sts.

Cont straight until left front matches back to beg of armhole shaping, ending with a WS row.

Shape armhole

Cast off 5 (6: 6: 7: 7: 8) sts at beg of next row. 52 (54: 57: 59: 62: 64) sts.

Work 1 row.

Working all armhole decreases as set by back, dec 1 st at armhole edge of next 3 (3: 4: 4: 4: 4) rows. 49 (51: 53: 55: 58: 60) sts.

Work 1 (1: 0: 0: 0: 0) row, ending with a WS row.

Shape front slope

Working all front slope decreases in same way as armhole decreases, dec 1 st at armhole edge of next 1 (1: 1: 1: 3: 3) rows, then on foll 2 (3: 4: 5: 5: 6) alt rows, then on 2 foll 4th rows **and at same time** dec 1 st at front slope edge of next and foll 6 (7: 8: 8: 8: 8) alt

rows, then on foll 0 (0: 0: 0: 4th: 4th) row. 37 (37: 37: 38: 38: 39) sts.

Dec 1 st at front slope edge only on 2nd (2nd: 4th: 2nd: 4th: 2nd) and foll 0 (1: 0: 0: 0: 0) alt rows, then on every foll 4th row until 26 (26: 27: 28: 28: 29) sts rem.

Cont straight until left front matches back to start of shoulder shaping, ending with a WS row.

Shape shoulder

Cast off 9 (9: 9: 9: 9: 10) sts at beg of next and foll alt row.

Work 1 row.

Cast off rem 8 (8: 9: 10: 10: 9) sts.

RIGHT FRONT

Cast on 63 (67: 69: 73: 75: 79) sts using 3mm (US 2/3) needles and yarn A.

Work in moss st as given for back for 4 rows, ending with a WS row.

Row 5 (RS): Moss st 3 sts, work 2 tog, yrn (to make first buttonhole), moss st to end.

Work in moss st for a further 4 rows, ending with a RS row.

Row 10 (WS): (Inc in first st) 1 (0: 1: 0: 1: 0) times, moss st to last 7 sts and turn, leaving rem 7 sts on a holder. 57 (60: 63: 66: 69: 72) sts.

Change to 3¾mm (US 5) needles.

Beg with a K row, cont in st st, dec 1 st at end of 27th (29th: 29th: 29th: 29th: 29th) and every foll 10th row to 54 (57: 60: 63: 66: 69) sts, then on every foll 8th row until there are 52 (55: 58: 61: 64: 67) sts.

Complete to match left front, reversing shapings.

SLEEVES (both alike)

Cast on 57 (59: 59: 61: 63: 63) sts using 3mm (US 2/3) needles and yarn A.

Row 1 (RS): P0 (1: 1: 2: 3: 3), *K3, P3, rep from * to last 3 (4: 4: 5: 6: 6) sts, K3, P0 (1: 1: 2: 3: 3).

Row 2: K0 (1: 1: 2: 3: 3), *P3, K3, rep from * to last 3 (4: 4: 5: 6: 6) sts, P3, K0 (1: 1: 2: 3: 3).

These 2 rows form rib.

Cont in rib for a further 18 rows, ending with a WS row.

Change to 3¾mm (US 5) needles.

Beg with a K row, cont in st st, inc 1 st at each end of next and every foll 8th row to 69 (71: 81: 79: 81: 91) sts, then on every foll 10th (10th: 10th: 10th: 10th: -) row until there are 81 (83: 85: 87: 89: -) sts.

Cont straight until sleeve measures 45 (45: 45: 46: 46: 46)cm/17½ (17½: 17½: 18: 18: 18)in, ending with a WS row.

Shape top

Cast off 5 (6: 6: 7: 7: 8) sts at beg of next 2 rows. 71 (71: 73: 73: 75: 75) sts.

Working all decreases as set by back and front armholes, dec 1 st at each end of next 5 rows, then on foll 4 alt rows, then on every foll 4th row until 45 (45: 47: 47: 49: 49) sts rem.

Work 1 row, ending with a WS row.

Dec 1 st at each end of next and every foll alt row to 37 sts, then on foll 7 rows, ending with a WS row. Cast off rem 23 sts.

MAKING UP

PRESS as described on page 123.

Join both shoulder seams using backstitch, or mattress stitch if preferred.

Left front band

Slip 7 sts from left front holder onto 3mm (US 2/3) needles and rejoin yarn A with RS facing.

Cont in moss st until band, when slightly stretched, fits up left front opening edge, up left front slope and across to centre back neck, ending with a WS row.

Cast off in moss st.

Slip stitch band in place.

Mark positions for 6 buttons on this band – first to come level with buttonhole already worked in right front, last to come 1cm/½in below start of front slope shaping, and rem 4 buttons evenly spaced between.

Right front band

Slip 7 sts from right front holder onto 3mm (US 2/3) needles and rejoin yarn A with WS facing.

Cont in moss st until band, when slightly stretched, fits up right front opening edge, up right front slope and across to centre back neck, ending with a WS row and with the addition of a further 5 buttonholes worked as folls:

Buttonhole row (RS): Moss st 3 sts, work 2 tog, yrn (to make first buttonhole), moss st 2 sts.

When band is complete, cast off in moss st. Slip stitch band in place, joining ends of bands at centre back neck.

Flowers (make 13)

Flowers are worked using yarn B DOUBLE throughout. Before starting, thread 26 beads onto yarn B for each flower.

Cast on 41 sts using 3¾mm (US 5) needles and yarn B DOUBLE.

Row 1 (WS): K1, *make loop, K1, make beaded loop, K1, rep from * to end.

Row 2: Knit.

Row 3: K2, *make loop, K1, make beaded loop, K1, rep from * to last 3 sts, make loop, K2.

Row 4: (K2, K2tog) 10 times, K1. 31 sts.

Row 5: K1, *make loop, K1, make beaded loop, K1, rep from * to last 2 sts, make loop, K1.

Row 6: K1, (K2tog) 14 times, K2. 17 sts.

Row 7: As row 1.

Row 8: K1, (K2tog) 7 times, K2. 10 sts.

Row 9: (K2tog) 5 times.

Break yarn and thread through rem 5 sts. Pull up tight and fasten off securely.

Join row-ends of flower, then sew flowers to neck edge of garment as in photograph by attaching 5 or 6 beads at centre.

See page 124 for finishing instructions, setting in sleeves using the set-in method.

POODLE-COLLAR JACKET

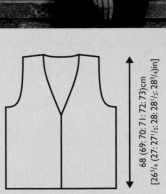

68 (69: 70: 71: 72: 73)cm
[26¾ (27: 27½: 28: 28½: 28¾)in]

57 (60: 62: 65.5: 67.5: 70.5)cm
[22½ (23½: 24½: 25½: 26½: 28)in]

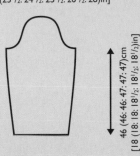

46 (46: 46: 47: 47: 47)cm
[18 (18: 18: 18½: 18½: 18½)in]

SIZES

1	2	3	4	5	6

TO FIT BUST

91	97	102	107	112	117	cm
36	38	40	42	44	46	in

YARN

Rowan Kid Classic – light aqua (822)

11	11	12	12	13	13 x 50gm

NEEDLES

1 pair 4mm (no 8) (US 6) needles
1 pair 4½mm (no 7) (US 7) needles
1 pair of 5mm (no 6) (US 8) needles

BUTTONS – 4

TENSION

19 sts and 25 rows to 10cm/4in measured over st st using 5mm (US 8) needles.

SPECIAL ABBREVIATIONS

make loop = K1 leaving st on left needle, bring yarn to front of work between needles and wrap it twice round thumb of left hand, take yarn back to WS of work between needles and K same st again, letting st slip off left needle, bring yarn to front of work between needles and take it back to WS over right needle point, lift last 2 sts on right needle over this loop and off right needle.

BACK

Cast on 108 (114: 118: 124: 128: 134) sts using 4mm (US 6) needles.
Row 1 (RS): K1 (0: 0: 1: 0: 0), P2 (2: 0: 2: 1: 0), *K2, P2, rep from * to last 1 (0: 2: 1: 3: 2) sts, K1 (0: 2: 1: 2: 2), P0 (0: 0: 0: 1: 0).
Row 2: P1 (0: 0: 1: 0: 0), K2 (2: 0: 2: 1: 0), *P2, K2, rep from * to last 1 (0: 2: 1: 3: 2) sts, P1 (0: 2: 1: 2: 2), K0 (0: 0: 0: 1: 0).
These 2 rows form rib.
Cont in rib for a further 16 rows, ending with a WS row.
Change to 5mm (US 8) needles.

Beg with a K row, cont in st st until back measures 45 (46: 46: 47: 47: 48)cm/17¾ (18: 18: 18½: 18¾: 19)in, ending with a WS row.
Shape armholes
Cast off 5 (6: 6: 7: 7: 8) sts at beg of next 2 rows. 98 (102: 106: 110: 114: 118) sts.
Next row (RS): K3, K2tog, K to last 5 sts, K2tog tbl, K3.
Next row: P3, P2tog tbl, P to last 5 sts, P2tog, P3.
Working all decreases as set by last 2 rows, dec 1 st at each end of next 3 (3: 5: 5: 7: 7) rows, then on foll 5 (6: 5: 6: 5: 6) alt rows, then on every foll 4th row until 74 (76: 78: 80: 82: 84) sts rem.
Cont straight until armhole measures 23 (23: 24: 24: 25: 25)cm/9 (9: 9½: 9½: 9¾: 9¾)in, ending with a WS row.
Shape shoulders and back neck
Cast off 7 (7: 8: 8: 8: 8) sts at beg of next 2 rows. 60 (62: 62: 64: 66: 68) sts.
Next row (RS): Cast off 7 (7: 8: 8: 8: 8) sts, K until there are 12 (12: 11: 12: 12: 13) sts on right needle and turn, leaving rem sts on a holder.
Work each side of neck separately.
Cast off 4 sts at beg of next row.
Cast off rem 8 (8: 7: 8: 8: 9) sts.
With RS facing, rejoin yarn to rem sts, cast off centre 22 (24: 24: 24: 26: 26) sts, K to end.
Complete to match first side, reversing shapings.

LEFT FRONT

Cast on 69 (72: 74: 77: 79: 82) sts using 4mm (US 6) needles.
Row 1 (RS): K1 (0: 0: 1: 0: 0), P2 (2: 0: 2: 1: 0), *K2, P2, rep from * to last 2 sts, K2.
Row 2: *P2, K2, rep from * to last 1 (0: 2: 1: 3: 2) sts, P1 (0: 2: 1: 2: 2), K0 (0: 0: 0: 1: 0).
These 2 rows form rib.
Cont in rib for a further 15 rows, ending with a RS row.
Row 18 (WS): Rib 14 and slip these sts onto a holder, rib to end. 55 (58: 60: 63: 65: 68) sts.

Change to 5mm (US 8) needles.
Beg with a K row, cont in st st until 18 rows less have been worked than on back to beg of armhole shaping, ending with a WS row.

Shape front slope
Dec 1 st at end of next and every foll 4th row until 50 (53: 55: 58: 60: 63) sts rem.
Work 1 row, ending with a WS row. (Left front should now match back to beg of armhole shaping.)

Shape armhole
Cast off 5 (6: 6: 7: 7: 8) sts at beg of next row. 45 (47: 49: 51: 53: 55) sts.
Work 1 row.
Working all armhole decreases as set by back, dec 1 st at armhole edge of next 5 (5: 7: 7: 9: 9) rows, then on foll 5 (6: 5: 6: 5: 6) alt rows, then on 2 foll 4th rows **and at same time** dec 1 st at front slope edge of next and every foll 4th row. 27 (27: 28: 29: 30: 30) sts.
Dec 1 st at front slope edge only on 2nd (4th: 4th: 2nd: 2nd: 4th) and every foll 6th (4th: 4th: 4th: 4th: 4th) row to 22 (24: 26: 27: 26: 27) sts, then on every foll - (6th: 6th: 6th: 6th: 6th) row until - (22: 23: 24: 24: 25) sts rem.
Cont straight until left front matches back to start of shoulder shaping, ending with a WS row.

Shape shoulder
Cast off 7 (7: 8: 8: 8: 8) sts at beg of next and foll alt row.
Work 1 row.
Cast off rem 8 (8: 7: 8: 8: 9) sts.

RIGHT FRONT
Cast on 69 (72: 74: 77: 79: 82) sts using 4mm (US 6) needles.
Row 1 (RS): *K2, P2, rep from * to last 1 (0: 2: 1: 3: 2) sts, K1 (0: 2: 1: 2: 2), P0 (0: 0: 0: 1: 0).
Row 2: P1 (0: 0: 1: 0: 0), K2 (2: 0: 2: 1: 0), *P2, K2, rep from * to last 2 sts, P2.
These 2 rows form rib.
Cont in rib for a further 6 rows, ending with a WS row.
Row 9 (buttonhole row) (RS): Rib 4, cast off 4 sts (to make a buttonhole – cast on 4 sts

over these cast-off sts on next row), rib to end.
Cont in rib for a further 8 rows, ending with a RS row.
Row 18 (WS): Rib to last 14 sts and turn, leaving rem 14 sts on a holder. 55 (58: 60: 63: 65: 68) sts.
Change to 5mm (US 8) needles.
Beg with a K row, cont in st st until 18 rows less have been worked than on back to beg of armhole shaping, ending with a WS row.

Shape front slope
Dec 1 st at beg of next and every foll 4th row until 50 (53: 55: 58: 60: 63) sts rem.
Complete to match left front, reversing shapings.

SLEEVES (both alike)
Cast on 44 (46: 46: 48: 50: 50) sts using 4mm (US 6) needles.
Row 1 (RS): P1 (0: 0: 1: 0: 0), *K2, P2, rep from * to last 3 (2: 2: 3: 2: 2) sts, K2, P1 (0: 0: 1: 0: 0).
Row 2: K1 (0: 0: 1: 0: 0), *P2, K2, rep from * to last 3 (2: 2: 3: 2: 2) sts, P2, K1 (0: 0: 1: 0: 0).
These 2 rows form rib.
Cont in rib for a further 16 rows, ending with a WS row.
Change to 5mm (US 8) needles.
Beg with a K row, cont in st st, shaping sides by inc 1 st at each end of next and every foll 6th (6th: 6th: 6th: 6th: 4th) row to 66 (68: 76: 74: 76: 54) sts, then on every foll 8th (8th: -: 8th: 8th: 6th) row until there are 72 (74: -: 78: 80: 82) sts.
Cont straight until sleeve measures 46 (46: 46: 47: 47: 47)cm/18 (18: 18: 18½: 18½: 18½)in, ending with a WS row.

Shape top
Cast off 5 (6: 6: 7: 7: 8) sts at beg of next 2 rows. 62 (62: 64: 64: 66: 66) sts.
Working all decreases as set by armholes, dec 1 st at each end of next 7 rows, then on foll 5 alt rows, then on every foll 4th row until 34 (34: 36: 36: 38: 38) sts rem.
Work 1 row, ending with a WS row.

Dec 1 st at each end of next and every foll alt row to 26 sts, then on foll 3 rows, ending with a WS row.
Cast off rem 20 sts.

MAKING UP
PRESS as described on page 123.
Join both shoulder seams using backstitch, or mattress stitch if preferred.

Left front band
Slip 14 sts from left front holder onto 4mm (US 6) needles and rejoin yarn with RS facing.
Cont in rib as set until band, when slightly stretched, fits up left front opening edge to start of front slope shaping, ending with a WS row.
Cast off in rib.
Slip stitch band in place.
Mark positions for 4 buttons on this band – first to come level with buttonhole already worked in right front, last to come 1cm/½in below start of front slope shaping, and rem 2 buttons evenly spaced between.

Right front band
Slip 14 sts from right front holder onto 4mm (US 6) needles and rejoin yarn with WS facing.
Cont in rib as set until band, when slightly stretched, fits up right front opening edge to start of front slope shaping, ending with a WS row and with the addition of a further 3 buttonholes to correspond with positions marked for buttons worked as folls:
Buttonhole row (RS): Rib 4, cast off 4 sts (to make a buttonhole – cast on 4 sts over these cast-off sts on next row), rib to end.
When band is complete, cast off in rib.
Slip stitch band in place.

Collar
Cast on 7 sts using 4½mm (US 7) needles.
Row 1 (WS): Knit.
Row 2: Inc in first st, *make loop, K1, rep from * to end. 8 sts.
Row 3: Knit.
Row 4: Inc in first st, *make loop, K1, rep from * to last st, K1. 9 sts.
Rows 5 to 8: As rows 1 to 4. 11 sts.

Row 9: K to last st, inc in last st. 12 sts.
Row 10: Inc in first st, K1, *make loop, K1, rep from * to end. 13 sts.
Row 11: As row 9. 14 sts.
Row 12: As row 4. 15 sts.
Rows 13 to 20: As rows 9 to 12, twice. 23 sts.
Rows 21 to 40: As rows 1 to 4, 5 times. 33 sts.
Row 41: Knit.
Row 42: K1, *make loop, K1, rep from * to end.
Row 43: Knit.
Row 44: K2, *make loop, K1, rep from * to last st, K1.
Last 4 rows form loop patt.
Cont in loop patt until collar measures 72 (74: 76: 76: 80: 80)cm/28¼ (29: 30: 30: 31½: 31½)in, ending with a RS row.
Keeping loop patt correct, dec 1 st at shaped edge of next and every foll alt row to 21 sts, then on foll 11 rows, then on foll 3 alt rows, ending with a RS row.
Cast off rem 7 sts.
Sew cast-on and cast-off ends of collar to top of front bands, and straight row-end edge of collar to front slope and back neck edges.
See page 124 for finishing instructions, setting in sleeves using the set-in method.

LACE-SLEEVE SWEATER

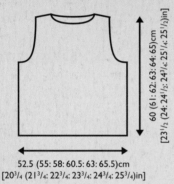

60 (61: 62: 63: 64: 65)cm
[23¹/₂ (24: 24¹/₂: 24³/₄: 25¹/₄: 25¹/₂)in]

52.5 (55: 58: 60.5: 63: 65.5)cm
[20³/₄ (21³/₄: 22³/₄: 23³/₄: 24³/₄: 25³/₄)in]

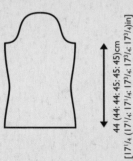

44 (44: 44: 45: 45: 45)cm
[17¹/₄ (17¹/₄: 17¹/₄: 17³/₄: 17³/₄: 17³/₄)in]

SIZES

1	2	3	4	5	6

TO FIT BUST

| 91 | 97 | 102 | 107 | 112 | 117 | cm |
| 36 | 38 | 40 | 42 | 44 | 46 | in |

YARN

Rowan Cotton Glace – black (727)

| 13 | 14 | 14 | 15 | 16 | 16 x 50gm |

NEEDLES

1 pair 2¾mm (no 12) (US 2) needles
1 pair 3¼mm (no 10) (US 3) needles
2¾mm (no 12) (US 2) circular needle
2 double-pointed 2¾mm (no 12) (US 2) needles

TENSION

23 sts and 32 rows to 10cm/4in measured over st st, 22 sts and 36 rows to 10cm/4in measured over lace pattern using 3¼mm (US 3) needles.

BACK

Cast on 121 (127: 133: 139: 145: 151) sts using 2¾mm (US 2) needles.
Work in garter st for 8 rows, ending with a WS row.
Change to 3¼mm (US 3) needles.
Row 5 (RS): Knit.
Row 6: K5, P to last 5 sts, K5.
Rep last 2 rows 12 times more, ending with a WS row.
Beg with a K row, cont in st st until back measures 37 (38: 38: 39: 39: 40)cm/14½ (15: 15: 15¼: 15½: 15¾)in from fold line row, ending with a WS row.
Shape armholes
Cast off 6 (7: 7: 8: 8: 9) sts at beg of next 2 rows. 109 (113: 119: 123: 129: 133) sts.
Dec 1 st at each end of next 5 (5: 7: 7: 9: 9) rows, then on foll 4 (5: 5: 6: 6: 7) alt rows, then on every foll 4th row until 87 (89: 91: 93: 95: 97) sts rem.
Cont straight until armhole measures 23 (23:

24: 24: 25: 25)cm/9 (9: 9½: 9½: 9¾: 9¾)in, ending with a WS row.
Shape shoulders and back neck
Cast off 6 (6: 6: 7: 7: 7) sts at beg of next 2 rows. 75 (77: 79: 79: 81: 83) sts.
Next row (RS): Cast off 6 (6: 6: 7: 7: 7) sts, K until there are 10 (10: 11: 10: 10: 11) sts on right needle and turn, leaving rem sts on a holder.
Work each side of neck separately.
Cast off 4 sts at beg of next row.
Cast off rem 6 (6: 7: 6: 6: 7) sts.
With RS facing, rejoin yarn to rem sts, cast off centre 43 (45: 45: 45: 47: 47) sts, K to end.
Complete to match first side, reversing shapings.

FRONT

Work as given for back until 10 (12: 12: 12: 12: 12) rows less have been worked than on back to start of shoulder shaping, ending with a WS row.
Shape neck
Next row (RS): K32 (33: 34: 35: 35: 36) and turn, leaving rem sts on a holder.
Work each side of neck separately.
Cast off 5 sts at beg of next and foll alt row. 22 (23: 24: 25: 25: 26) sts.
Dec 1 st at neck edge of next 3 rows, then on foll 1 (2: 2: 2: 2: 2) alt rows. 18 (18: 19: 20: 20: 21) sts.
Work 1 row, ending with a WS row.
Shape shoulder
Cast off 6 (6: 6: 7: 7: 7) sts at beg of next and foll alt row.
Work 1 row.
Cast off rem 6 (6: 7: 6: 6: 7) sts.
With RS facing, rejoin yarn to rem sts, cast off centre 23 (23: 23: 23: 25: 25) sts, K to end.
Complete to match first side, reversing shapings.

SLEEVES (both alike)

Cast on 85 (87: 87: 89: 91: 91) sts using 2¾mm (US 2) needles.
Beg with a K row, work in st st for 3 rows.

Row 4 (WS): Knit (to form fold line).
Beg with a K row, work in st st for 3 rows, ending with a RS row.
Row 8 (WS): P10, P2tog, *P19 (20: 20: 20: 21: 21), P2tog, rep from * twice more, P to end. 81 (83: 83: 85: 87: 87) sts.
Change to 3¼mm (US 3) needles.
Cont in lace patt as folls:
Row 1 (RS): K0 (1: 1: 2: 1: 1), (yfwd, sl 1, K1, psso) 0 (0: 0: 0: 1: 1) times, *K1, (K2tog, yfwd) twice, K1, (yfwd, sl 1, K1, psso) twice, rep from * to last 1 (2: 2: 3: 4: 4) sts, K1 (2: 2: 3: 1: 1), (K2tog, yfwd, K1) 0 (0: 0: 0: 1: 1) times.
Row 2: Purl.
Row 3: K0 (1: 1: 1: 2: 2), (yfwd, sl 1, K2tog, psso, yfwd) 0 (0: 0: 1: 1: 1) times, (K2tog, yfwd) 2 (2: 2: 1: 1: 1) times, K3, *yfwd, sl 1, K1, psso, yfwd, sl 1, K2tog, psso, yfwd, K2tog, yfwd, K3, rep from * to last 4 (5: 5: 6: 7: 7) sts, (yfwd, sl 1, K1, psso) 2 (2: 2: 1: 1: 1) times, (yfwd, sl 1, K2tog, psso, yfwd) 0 (0: 0: 1: 1: 1) times, K0 (1: 1: 1: 2: 2).
Row 4: Purl.
These 4 rows form lace patt.
Cont in lace patt, dec 1 st at each end of 5th and every foll 8th row to 71 (73: 73: 75: 77: 77) sts, then on every foll 10th row until 65 (67: 67: 69: 71: 71) sts rem.
Work 9 rows, ending with a WS row.
Inc 1 st at each end of next and every foll 8th (8th: 6th: 6th: 6th: 4th) row to 81 (83: 85: 83: 93: 79) sts, then on every foll – (-: 8th: 8th: -: 6th) row until there are - (-: 87: 89: -: 95) sts, taking inc sts into patt.
Cont straight until sleeve measures 44 (44: 44: 45: 45: 45)cm/17¼ (17¼: 17¼: 17¾: 17¾: 17¾)in from fold line row, ending with a WS row.
Shape top
Keeping patt correct, cast off 6 (7: 7: 8: 8: 9) sts at beg of next 2 rows. 69 (69: 73: 73: 77: 77) sts.
Dec 1 st at each end of next 7 rows, then on foll alt row to 49 sts, then on every foll 4th row until 33 sts rem.
Work 1 row, ending with a WS row.

Dec 1 st at each end of next and foll alt row, then on foll 3 rows, ending with a WS row.
Cast off rem 23 sts.

MAKING UP
PRESS as described on page 123.
Join both shoulder seams using backstitch, or mattress stitch if preferred.
Place marker on centre front neck st.
Neckband
With RS facing and using 2¾mm (US 2) circular needle, starting and ending at marked centre front neck st, pick up and knit 11 (11: 11: 11: 12: 12) sts from right section of cast-off neck sts, 17 (19: 19: 19: 19: 19) sts up right side of neck, 50 (52: 52: 52: 54: 54) sts from back, 17 (19: 19: 19: 19: 19) sts down left side of neck, then 11 (11: 11: 11: 12: 12) sts from left section of cast-off neck sts. 106 (112: 112: 112: 116: 116) sts.
Working backwards and forwards in rows, not rounds, cont as folls:
Beg with a P row, work in st st for 3 rows.
Row 4 (RS): Purl (to form fold line).
Beg with a P row, work in st st for 3 rows, ending with a WS row.
Cast off.
Neck tie
With 2¾mm (US 2) double-pointed needles, cast on 3 sts.
Row 1 (RS): K3, *without turning work push, these 3 sts to opposite end of needle and bring yarn to opposite end of work, pulling it quite tightly across back of these 3 sts. Using other needle, K these 3 sts again; rep from * until tie is 88cm/35in long.
Cast off.
Cuff ties (make 2)
Work as given for neck tie until cuff tie is 78cm/31in long.
Cast off.
See page 124 for finishing instructions, setting in sleeves using the set-in method and leaving side seams open for first 34 rows, and sleeve seams open for first 7 rows.
Fold first 3 rows of body and sleeves, and last

3 rows of neckband, to inside along fold line rows and slip stitch in place. Thread ties through these casings.

CABLE-YOKE JACKET

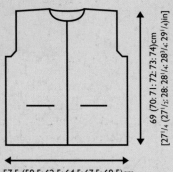

69 (70: 71: 72: 73: 74)cm
[27¼ (27½: 28: 28¼: 28¾: 29¼)in]

57.5 (59.5: 62.5: 64.5: 67.5: 69.5)cm
[22½ (23½: 24½: 25½: 26½: 27½)in]

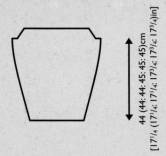

44 (44: 44: 45: 45: 45)cm
[17¼ (17¼: 17¼: 17¾: 17¾: 17¾)in]

SIZES

1	2	3	4	5	6

TO FIT BUST

| 91 | 97 | 102 | 107 | 112 | 117 | cm |
| 36 | 38 | 40 | 42 | 44 | 46 | in |

YARN

Rowan Denim – navy (225)

25	26	27	28	29	30 x 50gm

NEEDLES

1 pair 3¼mm (no 10) (US 3) needles
1 pair 4mm (no 8) (US 6) needles
2 double-pointed 3¼mm (no 10) (US 3) needles
Cable needle

BUTTONS – 7

TENSION

Before washing: 20 sts and 28 rows to 10cm/4in measured over st st using 4mm (US 6) needles.

Tension note: Denim will shrink in length when washed for the first time. Allowances have been made in the pattern for shrinkage (see size diagram for after washing measurements).

SPECIAL ABBREVIATIONS

C6B = slip next 3 sts onto cable needle and leave at back of work, K3, then K3 from cable needle.
C6F = slip next 3 sts onto cable needle and leave at front of work, K3, then K3 from cable needle.

BACK

Tassels
Cast on 3 sts using double-pointed 3¼mm (US 3) needles.
Row 1 (RS): K3, *without turning slip these 3 sts to opposite end of needle and bring yarn to opposite end of work pulling it quite tightly

across WS of work, K these 3 sts again, rep from * until tassel is 12cm/4¾in long.
Break yarn and leave sts on a holder.
Make a further 36 (38: 40: 42: 44: 46) tassels in this way.

Main section
Using 3¼mm (US 3) needles, cast on 2 (2: 1: 1: 0: 0) sts, (K across 3 tassel sts) 37 (39: 41: 43: 45: 47) times, cast on 2 (2: 1: 1: 0: 0) sts. 115 (121: 125: 131: 135: 141) sts.
Work in garter st for 11 rows, ending with a WS row.
Change to 4mm (US 6) needles.
Row 13 (RS): Knit.
Row 14: K6, P to last 6 sts, K6.
Rep last 2 rows 15 times more.
Beg with a K row, cont in st st until back measures 38 (39: 39: 40.5: 40.5: 41.5)cm/15 (15¼: 15¼: 16: 16: 16¼)in, ending with a WS row.
Work in garter st for 3 rows, ending with a RS row.
Next row (WS) (inc): K14 (17: 19: 22: 24: 27), *(K1, M1) 3 times, K9, rep from * 7 times more, K to end. 139 (145: 149: 155: 159: 165) sts.
Cont in cable patt as folls:
Row 1 (RS): K0 (1: 1: 0: 0: 1), (P1, K1) 7 (8: 9: 11: 12: 13) times, *K6, (K1, P1) 4 times, K1, rep from * 6 times more, K6, (K1, P1) 7 (8: 9: 11: 12: 13) times, K0 (1: 1: 0: 0: 1).
Row 2 and every foll alt row: K0 (1: 1: 0: 0: 1), (P1, K1) 7 (8: 9: 11: 12: 13) times, *P6, (K1, P1) 4 times, K1, rep from * 6 times more, P6, (K1, P1) 7 (8: 9: 11: 12: 13) times, K0 (1: 1: 0: 0: 1).
Row 3: K0 (1: 1: 0: 0: 1), (P1, K1) 7 (8: 9: 11: 12: 13) times, *C6B, (K1, P1) 4 times, K1, rep from * 3 times more, **C6F, (K1, P1) 4 times, K1, rep from ** twice more, C6F, (K1, P1) 7 (8: 9: 11: 12: 13) times, K0 (1: 1: 0: 0: 1).
Rows 5 and 7: As row 1.
Row 9: K0 (1: 1: 0: 0: 1), (P1, K1) 7 (8: 9: 11: 12: 13) times, *C6F, (K1, P1) 4 times, K1, rep from * 3 times more, **C6B, (K1, P1) 4 times, K1, rep from ** twice more, C6B, (K1, P1) 7 (8: 9: 11: 12: 13) times, K0 (1: 1: 0: 0: 1).

Row 11: As row 1.
Row 12: As row 2.
These 12 rows form patt.
Cont in patt until back measures 53.5 (55: 55: 56: 56: 57)cm/21 (21½: 21¾: 22: 22: 22¼)in, ending with a WS row.
Shape armholes
Keeping patt correct, cast off 6 sts at beg of next 2 rows. 127 (133: 137: 143: 147: 153) sts.
Dec 1 st at each end of next and foll 5 alt rows. 115 (121: 125: 131: 135: 141) sts.
Cont straight until armhole measures 27 (27: 28: 28: 29: 29)cm/10¾ (10¾: 11: 11: 11½: 11½)in, ending with a WS row.
Shape shoulders and back neck
Cast off 13 (14: 14: 15: 16: 17) sts at beg of next 2 rows. 89 (93: 97: 101: 103: 107) sts.
Next row (RS): Cast off 13 (14: 14: 15: 16: 17) sts, patt until there are 17 (17: 19: 20: 19: 20) sts on right needle and turn, leaving rem sts on a holder.
Work each side of neck separately.
Cast off 4 sts at beg of next row.
Cast off rem 13 (13: 15: 16: 15: 16) sts.
With RS facing, rejoin yarn to rem sts, cast off centre 29 (31: 31: 31: 33: 33) sts, patt to end.
Complete to match first side, reversing shapings.

POCKET LININGS (make 2)
Cast on 33 sts using 4mm (US 6) needles.
Beg with a K row, work in st st for 50 rows, ending with a WS row.
Break yarn and leave sts on a holder.

LEFT FRONT
Tassels
Make 21 (22: 23: 24: 25: 26) tassels as given for back.
Main section
Using 3¼mm (US 3) needles, cast on 2 (2: 1: 1: 0: 0) sts, (K across 3 tassel sts) 21 (22: 23: 24: 25: 26) times, cast on 1 st. 66 (69: 71: 74: 76: 79) sts.
Work in garter st for 10 rows, ending with a RS row.

Row 12 (WS): K8 and slip these sts onto a holder, K to end. 58 (61: 63: 66: 68: 71) sts.
Change to 4mm (US 6) needles.
Row 13 (RS): Knit.
Row 14: P to last 6 sts, K6.
Rep last 2 rows 15 times more.
Beg with a K row, work in st st for 18 rows, ending with a WS row.
Place pocket
Next row (RS): K12 (14: 15: 16: 17: 19), slip next 33 sts onto a holder and, in their place, K across 33 sts of first pocket lining, K to end.
Cont in st st until left front measures 38 (39: 39: 40.5: 40.5: 41.5)cm/15 (15¼: 15¼: 16: 16: 16¼)in, ending with a WS row.
Work in garter st for 3 rows, ending with a RS row.
Next row (WS) (inc): K5, *(K1, M1) 3 times, K9, rep from * 3 times more, K to end. 70 (73: 75: 78: 80: 83) sts.
Cont in cable patt as folls:
Row 1 (RS): K0 (1: 1: 0: 0: 1), (P1, K1) 7 (8: 9: 11: 12: 13) times, *K6, (K1, P1) 4 times, K1, rep from * twice more, K6, (K1, P1) twice, K1.
Row 2 and every foll alt row: K1, (P1, K1) twice, *P6, (K1, P1) 4 times, K1, rep from * twice more, P6, (K1, P1) 7 (8: 9: 11: 12: 13) times, K0 (1: 1: 0: 0: 1).
Row 3: K0 (1: 1: 0: 0: 1), (P1, K1) 7 (8: 9: 11: 12: 13) times, *C6B, (K1, P1) 4 times, K1, rep from * twice more, C6B, (K1, P1) twice, K1.
Rows 5 and 7: As row 1.
Row 9: K0 (1: 1: 0: 0: 1), (P1, K1) 7 (8: 9: 11: 12: 13) times, *C6F, (K1, P1) 4 times, K1, rep from * twice more, C6F, (K1, P1) twice, K1.
Row 11: As row 1.
Row 12: As row 2.
These 12 rows form patt.
Cont in patt until left front matches back to beg of armhole shaping, ending with a WS row.
Shape armhole
Keeping patt correct, cast off 6 sts at beg of next row. 64 (67: 69: 72: 74: 77) sts.
Work 1 row.
Dec 1 st at armhole edge of next and foll 5 alt

rows. 58 (61: 63: 66: 68: 71) sts.
Cont straight until 15 (17: 17: 17: 17: 17) rows less have been worked than on back to start of shoulder shaping, ending with a RS row.
Shape neck
Keeping patt correct, cast off 9 (9: 9: 9: 10: 10) sts at beg of next row. 49 (52: 54: 57: 58: 61) sts.
Dec 1 st at neck edge of next 8 rows, then on foll 1 (2: 2: 2: 2: 2) alt rows, then on foll 4th row, ending with a WS row. 39 (41: 43: 46: 47: 50) sts.
Shape shoulder
Cast off 13 (14: 14: 15: 16: 17) sts at beg of next and foll alt row.
Work 1 row.
Cast off rem 13 (13: 15: 16: 15: 16) sts.

RIGHT FRONT
Tassels
Make 21 (22: 23: 24: 25: 26) tassels as given for back.
Main section
Using 3¼mm (US 3) needles, cast on 1 st, (K across 3 tassel sts) 21 (22: 23: 24: 25: 26) times, cast on 2 (2: 1: 1: 0: 0) sts. 66 (69: 71: 74: 76: 79) sts.
Work in garter st for 10 rows, ending with a RS row.
Row 12 (WS): K to last 8 sts and turn, leaving rem 8 sts on a holder. 58 (61: 63: 66: 68: 71) sts.
Change to 4mm (US 6) needles.
Row 13 (RS): Knit.
Row 14: K6, P to end.
Rep last 2 rows 15 times more.
Beg with a K row, work in st st for 18 rows, ending with a WS row.
Place pocket
Next row (RS): K13 (14: 15: 17: 18: 19), slip next 33 sts onto a holder and, in their place, K across 33 sts of second pocket lining, K to end.
Cont in st st until right front measures 38 (39: 39: 40.5: 40.5: 41.5)cm/15 (15¼: 15¼: 16: 16: 16¼)in, ending with a WS row.

Work in garter st for 3 rows, ending with a RS row.

Next row (WS) (inc): K14 (17: 19: 22: 24: 27), *(K1, M1) 3 times, K9, rep from * twice more, (K1, M1) 3 times, K to end. 70 (73: 75: 78: 80: 83) sts.

Cont in cable patt as folls:

Row 1 (RS): K1, (P1, K1) twice, *K6, (K1, P1) 4 times, K1, rep from * twice more, K6, (K1, P1) 7 (8: 9: 11: 12: 13) times, K0 (1: 1: 0: 0: 1).

Row 2 and every foll alt row: K0 (1: 1: 0: 0: 1), (P1, K1) 7 (8: 9: 11: 12: 13) times, *P6, (K1, P1) 4 times, K1, rep from * twice more, P6, (K1, P1) twice, K1.

Row 3: K1, (P1, K1) twice, *C6F, (K1, P1) 4 times, K1, rep from * twice more, C6F, (K1, P1) 7 (8: 9: 11: 12: 13) times, K0 (1: 1: 0: 0: 1).

Rows 5 and 7: As row 1.

Row 9: K1, (P1, K1) twice, *C6B, (K1, P1) 4 times, K1, rep from ** twice more, C6B, (K1, P1) 7 (8: 9: 11: 12: 13) times, K0 (1: 1: 0: 0: 1).

Row 11: As row 1.

Row 12: As row 2.

These 12 rows form patt.

Complete to match left front, reversing shapings.

SLEEVES (both alike)

Cast on 53 (55: 55: 57: 59: 59) sts using 3¼mm (US 3) needles.

Work in garter st for 12 rows, ending with a WS row.

Change to 4mm (US 6) needles.

Beg with a K row, cont in st st, inc 1 st at each end of next and every foll 6th (6th: 4th: 6th: 6th: 6th) row to 83 (83: 59: 87: 89: 89) sts, then on every foll - (-: 6th: -: -: -) row until there are - (-: 85: -: -: -) sts.

Work 1 (7: 3: 1: 1: 1) rows, ending with a WS row.

Work in garter st for 3 rows, inc 0 (1: 1: 0: 0: 0) st at each end of 0 (first: 3rd: 0: 0: 0) of these rows and ending with a RS row. 83 (85: 87: 87: 89: 89) sts.

Next row (WS) (inc): K22 (23: 24: 24: 25: 25), *(K1, M1) 3 times, K9, rep from * twice more, (K1, M1) 3 times, K to end. 95 (97: 99: 99: 101: 101) sts.

Cont in cable patt as folls:

Row 1 (RS): (Inc in first st) 1 (0: 0: 1: 1: 1) times, K1 (1: 0: 1: 0: 0), (P1, K1) 10 (11: 12: 11: 12: 12) times, *K6, (K1, P1) 4 times, K1, rep from * twice more, K6, (K1, P1) 10 (11: 12: 11: 12: 12) times, K1 (1: 0: 1: 0: 0), (inc in last st) 1 (0: 0: 1: 1: 1) times. 97 (97: 99: 101: 103: 103) sts.

Row 2: K1 (1: 0: 1: 0: 0), (P1, K1) 11 (11: 12: 12: 13: 13) times, *P6, (K1, P1) 4 times, K1, rep from * twice more, P6, (K1, P1) 11 (11: 12: 12: 13: 13) times, K1 (1: 0: 1: 0: 0).

Row 3: K1 (1: 0: 1: 0: 0), (P1, K1) 11 (11: 12: 12: 13: 13) times, *C6B, (K1, P1) 4 times, K1, rep from * once more, C6F, (K1, P1) 4 times, K1, C6B, (K1, P1) 11 (11: 12: 12: 13: 13) times, K1 (1: 0: 1: 0: 0).

Row 4: As row 2.

Row 5: (Inc in first st) 0 (1: 1: 0: 0: 0) times, K1 (0: 1: 1: 0: 0), (P1, K1) 11 (11: 11: 12: 13: 13) times, *K6, (K1, P1) 4 times, K1, rep from * twice more, K6, (K1, P1) 11 (11: 11: 12: 13: 13) times, K1 (0: 1: 1: 0: 0), (inc in last st) 0 (1: 1: 0: 0: 0) times. 97 (99: 101: 101: 103: 103) sts.

Row 6: K1 (0: 1: 1: 0: 0), (P1, K1) 11 (12: 12: 12: 13: 13) times, *P6, (K1, P1) 4 times, K1, rep from * twice more, P6, (K1, P1) 11 (12: 12: 12: 13: 13) times, K1 (0: 1: 1: 0: 0).

Row 7: (Inc in first st) 1 (0: 0: 1: 1: 1) times, K0 (0: 1: 0: 1: 1), (P1, K1) 11 (12: 12: 12: 12: 12) times, *K6, (K1, P1) 4 times, K1, rep from * twice more, K6, (K1, P1) 11 (12: 12: 12: 12: 12) times, K0 (0: 1: 0: 1: 1), (inc in last st) 1 (0: 0: 1: 1: 1) times. 99 (99: 101: 103: 105: 105) sts.

Row 8: K0 (0: 1: 0: 1: 1), (P1, K1) 12 (12: 12: 13: 13: 13) times, *P6, (K1, P1) 4 times, K1, rep from * twice more, P6, (K1, P1) 12 (12: 12: 13: 13: 13) times, K0 (0: 1: 0: 1: 1).

Row 9: K0 (0: 1: 0: 1: 1), (P1, K1) 12 (12: 12: 13: 13: 13) times, *C6F, (K1, P1) 4 times, K1, rep from * once more, C6B, (K1, P1) 4 times, K1, C6B, (K1, P1) 12 (12: 12: 13: 13: 13) times, K0 (0: 1: 0: 1: 1).

Row 10: As row 8.

Row 11: (Inc in first st) 0 (0: 1: 0: 0: 0) times, K0 (0: 0: 0: 1: 1), (P1, K1) 12 (12: 12: 13: 13: 13) times, *K6, (K1, P1) 4 times, K1, rep from * twice more, K6, (K1, P1) 12 (12: 12: 13: 13: 13) times, K0 (0: 0: 0: 1: 1), (inc in last st) 0 (0: 1: 0: 0: 0) times. 99 (99: 103: 103: 105: 105) sts.

Row 12: K0 (0: 0: 0: 1: 1), (P1, K1) 12 (12: 13: 13: 13: 13) times, *P6, (K1, P1) 4 times, K1, rep from * twice more, P6, (K1, P1) 12 (12: 13: 13: 13: 13) times, K0 (0: 0: 0: 1: 1).

These 12 rows form patt and cont sleeve shaping.

Cont in patt, shaping sides by inc 1 st at each end of next (next: 5th: 3rd: next: next) and every foll 8th (8th: 6th: 8th: 6th: 6th) row until there are 105 (105: 109: 109: 113: 113) sts, taking inc sts into moss st.

Cont straight until sleeve measures 51.5 (51.5: 51.5: 52.5: 52.5: 52.5)cm/20¼ (20¼: 20¼: 20¾: 20¾: 20¾)in, ending with a WS row.

Shape top

Keeping patt correct, cast off 6 sts at beg of next 2 rows. 93 (93: 97: 97: 101: 101) sts.

Dec 1 st at each end of next and foll 5 alt rows, then on foll row, ending with a WS row.

Cast off rem 79 (79: 83: 83: 87: 87) sts.

MAKING UP

Do NOT press.

Join both shoulder seams using backstitch, or mattress stitch if preferred.

Left front band

Slip 8 sts from left front holder onto 3¼mm (US 3) needles and rejoin yarn with RS facing.

Cont in garter st until band, when slightly stretched, fits up left front opening edge to neck shaping, ending with a WS row.

Break yarn and leave sts on a holder.

Slip stitch band in place.

Mark positions for 6 buttons on this band section – first to come 18cm/7in up from lower edge, last to come 1cm/½in below neck shaping, and rem 4 buttons evenly spaced between.

Right front band

Slip 8 sts from right front holder onto 3¼mm

(US 3) needles and rejoin yarn with WS facing. Cont in garter st until band, when slightly stretched, fits up right front opening edge to neck shaping, ending with a WS row and with the addition of 6 buttonholes worked as folls:

Buttonhole row (RS): K3, K2tog, yfwd (to make a buttonhole), K3.

When band is complete, do NOT break yarn. Slip stitch band in place.

Collar

With RS facing and using 3¼mm (US 3) needles, K 8 from right front band, pick up and knit 24 (26: 26: 26: 27: 27) sts up right side of neck, 31 (33: 33: 33: 34: 34) sts from back, and 24 (26: 26: 26: 27: 27) sts down left side of neck, then K 8 from left front band. 95 (101: 101: 101: 104: 104) sts.

Work in garter st for 3 rows, ending with a WS row.

Next row (RS of body): K3, K2tog, yfwd (to make 7th buttonhole), K to end.

Work in garter st for a further 4 rows.

Cast off 4 sts at beg of next 2 rows. 87 (93: 93: 93: 96: 96) sts.

Cont in garter st until collar measures 12cm/4¾in from pick-up row, ending with RS of collar (WS of body) facing for next row.

Using 3¼mm (US 3) double-pointed needles, work tassel cast-off as folls: K3, *(without turning slip these 3 sts to opposite end of needle and bring yarn to opposite end of work pulling it quite tightly across WS of work, K these 3 sts again) until tassel is 12cm/4¾in long, without turning slip these 3 sts to opposite end of needle and bring yarn to opposite end of work pulling it quite tightly across WS of work, K3tog and fasten off, K next 3 sts of collar, rep from * until all sts have been cast off.

Pocket tops (both alike)

Slip 33 sts from pocket holder onto 3¼mm (US 3) needles and rejoin yarn with RS facing. Work in garter st for 12 rows.

Cast off knitwise (on WS).

Machine wash all pieces before completing sewing together.

See page 124 for finishing instructions, setting in sleeves using the shallow set-in method and leaving side seams open for first 44 rows. Tie a knot in end of each tassel.

NATURAL COLOURS

This summery colour palette focuses on
soft creams and beiges, with the addition
of earth tones, to provide very wearable
and adaptable designs for all occasions,
including textured jackets, smart tops, a
range of traditional sweaters and even a
great poncho! The emphasis is on cotton
yarns in this section.

Right This little sleeveless Leaf-trim Vest, knitted in a lightweight cotton yarn, is ideal for summer. It has an attractive textured hem and soft cowl neckline. (Instructions on page 72).

Far right This cabled, edge to edge, hip-length Herringbone Jacket is knitted in a double-knitting weight merino wool. It makes the perfect summer cover-up, and is versatile enough to be dressed up for an evening out. (Instructions on page 76.)

Far left Another great classic cable design, this smart traditional Cable-trim Jacket is knitted in chunky merino wool. Wear it over a classic T-shirt or with the sleeveless tops shown centre and near left. (Instructions on page 80.)

Centre left With a row of little lace heart motifs above the ribbed hem and a knitted scalloped neck edging, the Lace-heart Vest would pair well with many of the jackets in the book. It is worked in a super-soft cotton yarn. (Instructions on page 74.)

Near left The Plain V-neck Top, also shown on page 60, is worked in a soft, lightweight merino wool. The round-neck version of this plain top is shown with the Mesh Scarf on page 105. (Instructions on page 78.)

Left A pretty edging around the neck, armholes and hem of the V-neck Top gives it a special finishing touch. (Instructions on page 78.)

Above (left to right) The Bobble-trim, Tassel-trim and Cable-trim Sweaters are variations on the classic off-white sweater, in three different cotton yarns.

All are easy-to-wear hip-length sweaters, with stylish finishing touches. (Instructions on page 82–86.)

Above *A clever variation on the classic afghan crochet square creates a smart bag and matching scarf (see opposite). In toning earth shades that harmonize well with most colours, the Motif Bag is a great project for both crochet lovers and those recently converted to the technique! (Instructions on page 88.)*

Above *Pair the Motif Scarf, worked in extra fine merino wool, with the matching bag or use it on its own to liven up a plain top or jacket. (Instructions on page 89.)*

Above *The Garter-rib Sweater is the warm, comfortable cotton knit we all want in our wardrobe, for walks in the country or for lounging by the fire. (Instructions on page 92.)*

Right *A must-have design and the world's greatest cover up! This classic Tweed Poncho is knitted in stocking stitch in a chunky wool-mix yarn. It features a cosy rolled collar and a stylish long fringed yoke and hem. (Instructions on page 94.)*

Left This smart little moss-stitch Bobble-trim Scarf, with its lacy crocheted bobble edging, is very quick and easy to work. Make it full length or as a short muffler. (Instructions on page 90.)

Above *In an extra-soft, lofty cotton-mix yarn, the Cabled Scarf is a popular classic. It also makes the ideal project for newcomers to cable knitting! (Instructions on page 91.)*

Above The Beaded Jacket above and the textured version on page 20 are both really versatile designs. Worked in extra fine merino, they can be worn with a skirt or smart pair of trousers to the office but are also ideal, as here, for country walks. (Instructions on page 96.)

Above: A classic polo-neck design, the Diamond-pattern Sweater is knitted in a lightweight merino wool. The textured pattern is worked from a chart and is formed with simple knit and purl stitches. (Instructions on page 100.)

Above: This retro-style Zigzag Scarf in four toning colours of soft merino wool is easier to make than it looks. The zigzag pattern stitch, with its very simple two-row repeat, is quickly memorized. (Instructions on page 95.)

LEAF-TRIM VEST

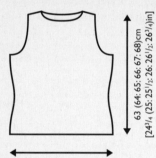

63 (64: 65: 66: 67: 68)cm
[24¾ (25: 25½: 26: 26½: 26¾)in]

50.5 (52.5: 55.5: 57.5: 60.5: 62.5)cm
[20 (20¾: 21¾: 22¾: 23¾: 24½)in]

SIZES

1	2	3	4	5	6

TO FIT BUST

91	97	102	107	112	117	cm
36	38	40	42	44	46	in

YARN

Rowan 4 ply Cotton – ecru (112)

7	8	8	9	9	10 x 50gm

NEEDLES

1 pair 2¼mm (no 13) (US 1) needles
1 pair 2¾mm (no 12) (US 2) needles
1 pair 3mm (no 11) (US 2/3) needles

TENSION

28 sts and 38 rows to 10cm/4in measured over st st using 3mm (US 2/3) needles.

BACK

Cast on 141 (147: 155: 161: 169: 175) sts using 2¼mm (US 1) needles.
Row 1 (RS): P0 (3: 0: 3: 0: 3), K1, *yfrn, P5, P3tog, P5, yon, K1, rep from * to last 0 (3: 0: 3: 0: 3) sts, P0 (3: 0: 3: 0: 3).
Row 2 and every foll alt row: Purl.
Rows 3, 5, 7, 9 and 11: As row 1.
Change to 2¾mm (US 2) needles.
Row 13: K1 (4: 1: 4: 1: 4), *yfwd, sl 1, K1, psso, yfrn, P3, P3tog, P3, yon, K2tog, yfwd, K1, rep from * to last 0 (3: 0: 3: 0: 3) sts, K0 (3: 0: 3: 0: 3).
Row 15: K1 (4: 1: 4: 1: 4), *yfwd, K1, sl 1, K1, psso, yfrn, P2, P3tog, P2, yon, K2tog, K1, yfwd, K1, rep from * to last 0 (3: 0: 3: 0: 3) sts, K0 (3: 0: 3: 0: 3).
Row 17: K1 (4: 1: 4: 1: 4), *yfwd, K2, sl 1, K1, psso, yfrn, P1, P3tog, P1, yon, K2tog, K2, yfwd, K1, rep from * to last 0 (3: 0: 3: 0: 3) sts, K0 (3: 0: 3: 0: 3).
Row 19: K1 (4: 1: 4: 1: 4), *yfwd, K3, sl 1, K1, psso, yfrn, P3tog, yon, K2tog, K3, yfwd, K1, rep from * to last 0 (3: 0: 3: 0: 3) sts, K0 (3: 0: 3: 0: 3).
Change to 3mm (US 2/3) needles.
Row 21: K1 (4: 1: 4: 1: 4), *K3, K2tog, yfwd, K3, yfwd, sl 1, K1, psso, K4, rep from * to last 0 (3: 0: 3: 0: 3) sts, K0 (3: 0: 3: 0: 3).
Row 23: K1 (4: 1: 4: 1: 4), *K2, K2tog, yfwd, K5, yfwd, sl 1, K1, psso, K3, rep from * to last 0 (3: 0: 3: 0: 3) sts, K0 (3: 0: 3: 0: 3).
Row 25: K1 (4: 1: 4: 1: 4), *K1, K2tog, yfwd, K7, yfwd, sl 1, K1, psso, K2, rep from * to last 0 (3: 0: 3: 0: 3) sts, K0 (3: 0: 3: 0: 3).
Row 27: K1 (4: 1: 4: 1: 4), *K2tog, yfwd, K9, yfwd, sl 1, K1, psso, K1, rep from * to last 0 (3: 0: 3: 0: 3) sts, K0 (3: 0: 3: 0: 3).
Row 29: K0 (3: 0: 3: 0: 3), K2tog, yfwd, *K11, yfwd, sl 1, K2tog, psso, yfwd, rep from * to last 13 (16: 13: 16: 13: 16) sts, K11, yfwd, sl 1, K1, psso, K0 (3: 0: 3: 0: 3).
Row 30: As row 2.
These 30 rows complete border patt.
Beg with a K row, cont in st st until back measures 10 (11: 11: 12: 12: 13)cm/4 (4¼: 4¼: 4¾: 5: 5¼)in, ending with a WS row.
Dec 1 st at each end of next and every foll 10th row until 129 (135: 143: 149: 157: 163) sts rem.
Work 9 rows, ending with a WS row.
Inc 1 st at each end of next and every foll 10th row until there are 141 (147: 155: 161: 169: 175) sts.
Cont straight until back measures 42 (43: 43: 44: 44: 45)cm/16½ (16¾: 16¾: 17¼: 17½: 17¾)in, ending with a WS row.
Shape armholes
Cast off 7 (8: 8: 9: 9: 10) sts at beg of next 2 rows. 127 (131: 139: 143: 151: 155) sts.
Dec 1 st at each end of next 9 (9: 11: 11: 13: 13) rows, then on foll 7 (8: 8: 9: 9: 10) alt rows, then on foll 4th row. 93 (95: 99: 101: 105: 107) sts.
Cont straight until armhole measures 21 (21: 22: 22: 23: 23)cm/8¼ (8¼: 8¾: 8¾: 9: 9)in, ending with a WS row.
Shape shoulders and back neck
Cast off 5 (5: 6: 6: 6: 7) sts at beg of next 2 rows. 83 (85: 87: 89: 93: 93) sts.
Next row (RS): Cast off 5 (5: 6: 6: 6: 7) sts, K until there are 9 (9: 9: 10: 11: 10) sts on right needle and turn, leaving rem sts on a holder.

Work each side of neck separately.

Cast off 4 sts at beg of next row.

Cast off rem 5 (5: 5: 6: 7: 6) sts.

With RS facing, rejoin yarn to rem sts, cast off centre 55 (57: 57: 57: 59: 59) sts, K to end.

Complete to match first side, reversing shapings.

FRONT

Work as given for back until 14 (16: 16: 16: 16: 16) rows less have been worked than on back to start of shoulder shaping, ending with a WS row.

Shape neck

Next row (RS): K27 (28: 30: 31: 32: 33) and turn, leaving rem sts on a holder.

Work each side of neck separately.

Cast off 5 sts at beg of next row. 22 (23: 25: 26: 27: 28) sts.

Dec 1 st at neck edge of next 3 rows, then on foll 4 (5: 5: 5: 5: 5) alt rows. 15 (15: 17: 18: 19: 20) sts.

Work 1 row, ending with a WS row.

Shape shoulder

Cast off 5 (5: 6: 6: 6: 7) sts at beg of next and foll alt row.

Work 1 row.

Cast off rem 5 (5: 5: 6: 7: 6) sts.

With RS facing, rejoin yarn to rem sts, cast off centre 39 (39: 39: 39: 41: 41) sts, K to end.

Complete to match first side, reversing shapings.

MAKING UP

PRESS as described on page 123.

Join both shoulder seams using backstitch, or mattress stitch if preferred.

Armhole borders (both alike)

With RS facing and using 2¼mm (US 1) needles, pick up and knit 130 (132: 138: 140: 146: 148) sts all round armhole edge.

Work in garter st for 2 rows.

Cast off knitwise (on WS).

Collar

Cast on 169 (169: 183: 183: 197: 197) sts using 2¼mm (US 1) needles.

Row 1 (RS): K1, *yfrn, P5, P3tog, P5, yon, K1, rep from * to end.

Row 2 and every foll alt row: Purl.

Rows 3, 5, 7, 9 and 11: As row 1.

Change to 2¾mm (US 2) needles.

Row 13: K1, *yfwd, sl 1, K1, psso, yfrn, P3, P3tog, P3, yon, K2tog, yfwd, K1, rep from * to end.

Row 15: K1, *yfwd, K1, sl 1, K1, psso, yfrn, P2, P3tog, P2, yon, K2tog, K1, yfwd, K1, rep from * to end.

Row 17: K1, *yfwd, K2, sl 1, K1, psso, yfrn, P1, P3tog, P1, yon, K2tog, K2, yfwd, K1, rep from * to end.

Row 19: K1, *yfwd, K3, sl 1, K1, psso, yfrn, P3tog, yon, K2tog, K3, yfwd, K1, rep from * to end.

Change to 3mm (US 2/3) needles.

Row 21: K1, *K3, K2tog, yfwd, K3, yfwd, sl 1, K1, psso, K4, rep from * to end.

Row 23: K1, *K2, K2tog, yfwd, K5, yfwd, sl 1, K1, psso, K3, rep from * to end.

Row 25: K1, *K1, K2tog, yfwd, K7, yfwd, sl 1, K1, psso, K2, rep from * to end.

Row 27: K1, *K2tog, yfwd, K9, yfwd, sl 1, K1, psso, K1, rep from * to end.

Row 29: K2tog, yfwd, *K11, yfwd, sl 1, K2tog, psso, yfwd, rep from * to last 13 sts, K11, yfwd, sl 1, K1, psso.

Row 30: As row 2.

These 30 rows complete border patt.

Beg with a K row, cont in st st for 16 rows, ending with a WS row.

Change to 2¾mm (US 2) needles.

Row 47 (RS): K8 (8: 9: 9: 10: 10), K2tog, *K4, K2tog, rep from * to last 9 (9: 10: 10: 11: 11) sts, K to end. 143 (143: 155: 155: 167: 167) sts.

Cont in st st until collar measures 17cm/6¾in, ending with a WS row.

Change to 2¼mm (US 1) needles.

Next row (RS): K8 (8: 9: 9: 10: 10), K2tog, *K3, K2tog, rep from * to last 8 (8: 9: 9: 10: 10) sts, K to end. 117 (117: 127: 127: 137: 137) sts.

Cont in st st until collar measures 24cm/9½in, ending with a WS row.

Cast off knitwise.

Join row-end edges of collar. Placing seam at centre back neck and easing in slight fullness, sew cast-off edge of collar to neck edge.

See page 124 for finishing instructions.

LACE-HEART VEST

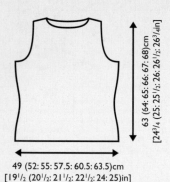

63 (64: 65: 66: 67: 68)cm
[24¾ (25: 25½: 26: 26½: 26¾)in]

49 (52: 55: 57.5: 60.5: 63.5)cm
[19½ (20½: 21½: 22½: 24: 25)in]

SIZES

| 1 | 2 | 3 | 4 | 5 | 6 | |

TO FIT BUST

| 91 | 97 | 102 | 107 | 112 | 117 | cm |
| 36 | 38 | 40 | 42 | 44 | 46 | in |

YARN

Rowan Calmer – coffee bean (481)

| 6 | 6 | 7 | 7 | 8 | 8 x 50gm |

NEEDLES

1 pair 4mm (no 8) (US 6) needles
1 pair 5mm (no 6) (US 8) needles

TENSION

21 sts and 30 rows to 10cm/4in measured over st st using 5mm (US 8) needles.

SPECIAL ABBREVIATION

dec2 = K2tog and slip st now on right needle back onto left needle, lift 2nd st on left needle over this st and off left needle, then slip same st back onto right needle.

BACK

Cast on 103 (109: 115: 121: 127: 133) sts using 4mm (US 6) needles.
Row 1 (RS): P2, *K3, P3, rep from * to last 5 sts, K3, P2.
Row 2: K2, *P3, K3, rep from * to last 5 sts, P3, K2.
These 2 rows form rib.
Work in rib for a further 4 rows, ending with a WS row.
Change to 5mm (US 8) needles.
Beg with a K row, work in st st for 4 rows, ending with a WS row.
Place heart motifs
Row 5 (RS): K5 (8: 3: 6: 1: 4), work next 13 sts as row 1 of heart motif chart, *K3, work next 13 sts as row 1 of heart motif chart, rep from * to last 5 (8: 3: 6: 1: 4) sts, K to end.
Row 6: P5 (8: 3: 6: 1: 4), work next 13 sts as row 2 of heart motif chart, *P3, work next 13

sts as row 2 of heart motif chart, rep from * to last 5 (8: 3: 6: 1: 4) sts, P to end.
These 2 rows set position of heart motifs on st st.
Cont as set until all 16 rows of heart motif chart have been completed, ending with a WS row.
Beg with a K row, cont in st st, dec 1 st at each end of 15th and every foll 12th row until 95 (101: 107: 113: 119: 125) sts rem.
Work 11 rows, ending with a WS row.
Inc 1 st at each end of next and every foll 10th row until there are 103 (109: 115: 121: 127: 133) sts.
Cont straight until back measures 42 (43: 43: 44: 44: 45)cm/16½ (16¾: 16¾: 17¼: 17½: 17¾)in, ending with a WS row.
Shape armholes
Cast off 6 (7: 7: 8: 8: 9) sts at beg of next 2 rows. 91 (95: 101: 105: 111: 115) sts.
Dec 1 st at each end of next 5 (5: 7: 7: 9: 9) rows, then on foll 4 (5: 5: 6: 6: 7) alt rows, then on every foll 4th row until 69 (71: 73: 75: 77: 79) sts rem.
Cont straight until armhole measures 21 (21: 22: 22: 23: 23)cm/8¼ (8¼: 8¾: 8¾: 9: 9)in, ending with a WS row.
Shape shoulders and back neck
Cast off 4 (4: 4: 5: 5: 5) sts at beg of next 2 rows. 61 (63: 65: 65: 67: 69) sts.
Next row (RS): Cast off 4 (4: 4: 5: 5: 5) sts, K until there are 8 (8: 9: 8: 8: 9) sts on right needle and turn, leaving rem sts on a holder.
Work each side of neck separately.
Cast off 4 sts at beg of next row.
Cast off rem 4 (4: 5: 4: 4: 5) sts.
With RS facing, rejoin yarn to rem sts, cast off centre 37 (39: 39: 39: 41: 41) sts, K to end.
Complete to match first side, reversing shapings.

FRONT

Work as given for back until 12 (14: 14: 14: 14: 14) rows less have been worked than on back to start of shoulder shaping, ending with a WS row.

Shape neck

Next row (RS): K24 (25: 26: 27: 27: 28) and turn, leaving rem sts on a holder.

Work each side of neck separately.

Cast off 5 sts at beg of next row. 19 (20: 21: 22: 22: 23) sts.

Dec 1 st at neck edge of next 5 rows, then on foll 2 (3: 3: 3: 3: 3) alt rows. 12 (12: 13: 14: 14: 15) sts.

Work 1 row, ending with a WS row.

Shape shoulder

Cast off 4 (4: 4: 5: 5: 5) sts at beg of next and foll alt row.

Work 1 row.

Cast off rem 4 (4: 5: 4: 4: 5) sts.

With RS facing, rejoin yarn to rem sts, cast off centre 21 (21: 21: 21: 23: 23) sts, K to end.

Complete to match first side, reversing shapings.

MAKING UP

PRESS as described on page 123.

Join both shoulder seams using backstitch.

Neck trim

Cast on 189 (200: 200: 200: 211: 211) sts using 4mm (US 6) needles.

Row 1 (WS): Purl.

Row 2: K2, *K1 and slip this st back onto left needle, lift the next 8 sts on left needle over this st and off left needle, (yfwd) twice, K st on left needle again, K2, rep from * to end.

Row 3: K1, *P2tog, (K1, K1 tbl) twice into double yfwd of previous row, P1, rep from * to last st, K1. 104 (110: 110: 110: 116: 116) sts.

Row 4: Knit.

Cast off knitwise.

Join row-end edges of neck trim, then sew cast-off edge of neck trim to neck edge, positioning seam at centre back neck.

Armhole borders (both alike)

With RS facing and using 4mm (US 6) needles, pick up and knit 100 (102: 106: 108: 112: 114) sts all round armhole edge.

Work in garter st for 2 rows.

Cast off knitwise (on WS).

See page 124 for finishing instructions.

Heart motif chart

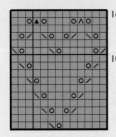

16

10

Key

☐ K on RS, P on WS

◙ yfwd

◩ sl1, K1, psso

◪ K2tog

◪ sl1, K2tog, psso

▲ dec 2

HERRINGBONE JACKET

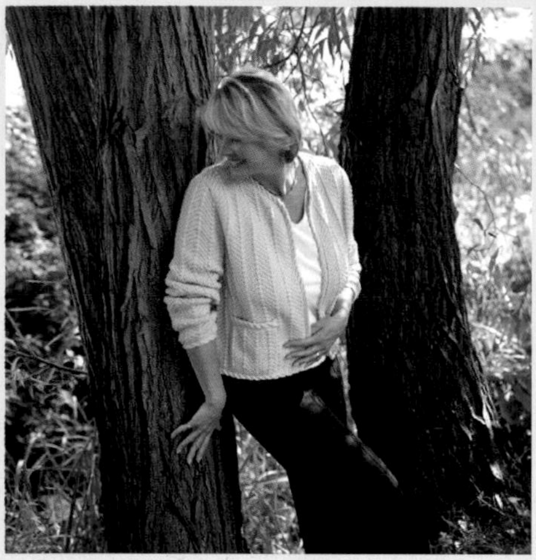

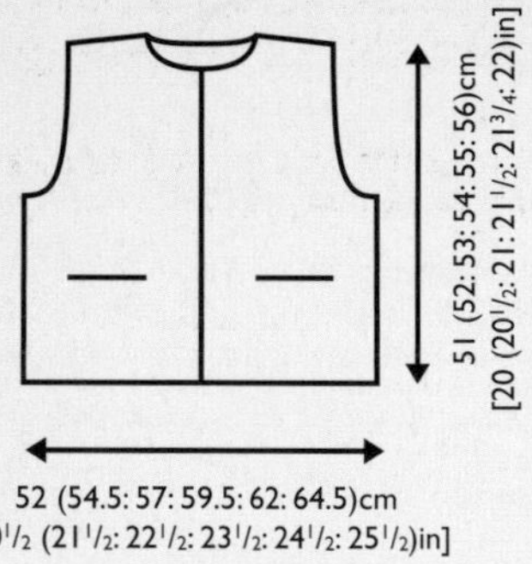
51 (52: 53: 54: 55: 56)cm
[20 (20½: 21: 21½: 21¾: 22)in]
52 (54.5: 57: 59.5: 62: 64.5)cm
[20½ (21½: 22½: 23½: 24½: 25½)in]

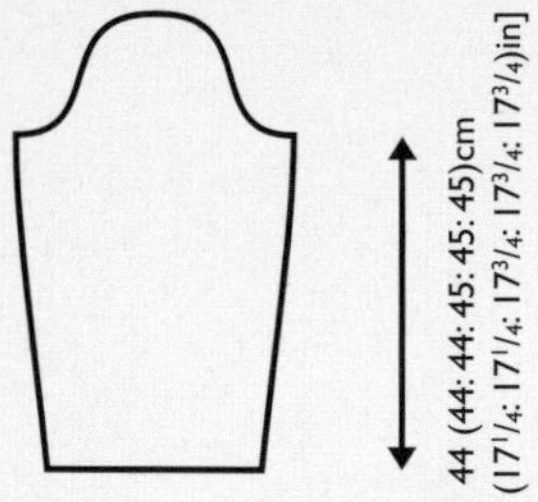
44 (44: 44: 45: 45: 45)cm
[17¼ (17¼: 17¼: 17¾: 17¾: 17¾)in]

SIZES

1	2	3	4	5	6	

TO FIT BUST

91	97	102	107	112	117	cm
36	38	40	42	44	46	in

YARN

Jaeger Extra Fine Merino DK –
oatmeal (936)

14	14	15	15	16	16 x 50gm

NEEDLES

1 pair 3mm (no 11) (US 2/3) needles
1 pair 3¾mm (no 9) (US 5) needles
Cable needle

TENSION

24 sts and 36 rows to 10cm/4in measured over pattern using 3¾mm (US 5) needles.

SPECIAL ABBREVIATIONS

C6B = slip next 3 sts onto cable needle and leave at back of work, K3, then K3 from cable needle.

BACK

Cast on 125 (131: 137: 143: 149: 155) sts using 3¾mm (US 5) needles.
Starting and ending rows as indicated and repeating the 4 row patt rep throughout, cont in patt from chart as folls:
Cont straight until back measures 26 (27: 27: 28: 28: 29)cm/10¼ (10¾: 10¾: 11¼: 11¼: 11½)in, ending with a WS row.

Shape armholes

Keeping patt correct, cast off 7 (8: 8: 9: 9: 10) sts at beg of next 2 rows. 111 (115: 121: 125: 131: 135) sts.
Dec 1 st at each end of next 3 (3: 5: 5: 7: 7) rows, then on foll 3 (4: 4: 5: 5: 6) alt rows, then on every foll 4th row until 95 (97: 99: 101: 103: 105) sts rem.
Cont straight until armhole measures 23 (23: 24: 24: 25: 25)cm/9 (9: 9½: 9½: 9¾: 9¾)in, ending with a WS row.

Shape shoulders and back neck

Cast off 9 (9: 10: 10: 10: 10) sts at beg of next 2 rows. 77 (79: 79: 81: 83: 85) sts.
Next row (RS): Cast off 9 (9: 10: 10: 10: 10) sts, patt until there are 14 (14: 13: 14: 14: 15) sts on right needle and turn, leaving rem sts on a holder.
Work each side of neck separately.
Cast off 4 sts at beg of next row.
Cast off rem 10 (10: 9: 10: 10: 11) sts.
With RS facing, rejoin yarn to rem sts, cast off centre 31 (33: 33: 33: 35: 35) sts, patt to end.
Complete to match first side, reversing shapings.

POCKET LININGS (make 2)

Cast on 29 sts using 3¾mm (US 5) needles.
Beg with a K row, work in st st for 40 rows, ending with a WS row.
Row 41 (RS): (K10, M1) twice, K9. 31 sts.
Break yarn and leave sts on a holder.

LEFT FRONT

Cast on 60 (63: 66: 69: 72: 75) sts using 3¾mm (US 5) needles.
Starting and ending rows as indicated, cont in patt from chart as folls:
Work 1 row.
Inc 1 st at beg of next row and at same edge on foll 2 rows. 63 (66: 69: 72: 75: 78) sts.
Cont straight for a further 42 rows, ending with a WS row.

Place pocket

Row 47 (RS): Patt 19 sts, cast off next 31 sts, patt to end.
Row 48: Patt 13 (16: 19: 22: 25: 28) sts, patt across 31 sts of first pocket lining, patt to end.
Cont straight until left front matches back to beg of armhole shaping, ending with a WS row.

Shape armhole

Keeping patt correct, cast off 7 (8: 8: 9: 9: 10) sts at beg of next row. 56 (58: 61: 63: 66: 68) sts.
Work 1 row.
Dec 1 st at armhole edge of next 3 (3: 5: 5: 7: 7) rows, then on foll 3 (4: 4: 5: 5: 6) alt rows,

then on every foll 4th row until 48 (49: 50: 51: 52: 53) sts rem.

Cont straight until 19 (21: 21: 21: 21: 21) rows less have been worked than on back to start of shoulder shaping, ending with a RS row.

Shape neck

Keeping patt correct, cast off 9 (9: 9: 9: 10: 10) sts at beg of next row. 39 (40: 41: 42: 42: 43) sts.

Dec 1 st at neck edge of next 6 rows, then on foll 4 (5: 5: 5: 5: 5) alt rows, then on foll 4th row, ending with a WS row. 28 (28: 29: 30: 30: 31) sts.

Shape shoulder

Cast off 9 (9: 10: 10: 10: 10) sts at beg of next and foll alt row.

Work 1 row.

Cast off rem 10 (10: 9: 10: 10: 11) sts.

RIGHT FRONT

Cast on 60 (63: 66: 69: 72: 75) sts using 3¾mm (US 5) needles.

Starting and ending rows as indicated, cont in patt from chart as folls:

Work 1 row.

Inc 1 st at end of next row and at same edge on foll 2 rows. 63 (66: 69: 72: 75: 78) sts.

Cont straight for a further 42 rows, ending with a WS row.

Place pocket

Row 47 (RS): Patt 13 (16: 19: 22: 25: 28) sts, cast off next 31 sts, patt to end.

Row 48: Patt 19 sts, patt across 31 sts of second pocket lining, patt to end.

Complete to match left front, reversing shapings.

SLEEVES (both alike)

Cast on 63 (65: 65: 67: 69: 69) sts using 3¾mm (US 5) needles.

Starting and ending rows as indicated, cont in patt from chart, inc 1 st at each end of 9th (9th: 7th: 7th: 7th: 7th) and every foll 10th (10th: 8th: 8th: 8th: 8th) row to 85 (87: 71: 71: 73: 83) sts, then on every foll 12th (12th: 10th: 10th: 10th: 10th) row until there are 89 (91: 93: 95: 97: 99) sts, taking inc sts into patt.

Cont straight until sleeve measures 42 (42: 42: 43: 43: 43)cm/16½ (16½: 16½: 17: 17: 17)in, ending with a WS row.

Shape top

Keeping patt correct, cast off 7 (8: 8: 9: 9: 10) sts at beg of next 2 rows. 75 (75: 77: 77: 79: 79) sts.

Dec 1 st at each end of next 5 rows, then on foll 4 alt rows, then on every foll 4th row until 43 (43: 45: 45: 47: 47) sts rem.

Work 1 row, ending with a WS row.

Dec 1 st at each end of next and every foll alt row to 35 sts, then on foll 5 rows, ending with a WS row.

Cast off rem 25 sts.

MAKING UP

PRESS as described on page 123.

Join both shoulder seams using backstitch, or mattress stitch if preferred. Join side seams.

Front edging

Cast on 8 sts using 3mm (US 2/3) needles.

Row 1 (RS): P2, K6.

Row 2: P6, K2.

Row 3: P2, C6B.

Row 4: As row 2.

Rows 5 and 6: As rows 1 and 2.

These 6 rows form patt.

Cont in patt until edging fits around entire hem, front opening and neck edges, starting and ending at base of left side seam, easing in fullness around corners to ensure edging lays flat and ending with a WS row.

Cast off.

Slip stitch un-cabled edge in place, joining cast-on and cast-off edges.

Cuff edging (both alike)

Work as given for front edging, working a strip long enough to fit along sleeve cast-on edge.

Pocket edgings (both alike)

Work as given for front edging, working a strip long enough to fit across cast-off edge of pocket opening.

See page 124 for finishing instructions, setting in sleeves using the set-in method.

Key □ K on RS, P on WS   ▣ P on RS, K on WS

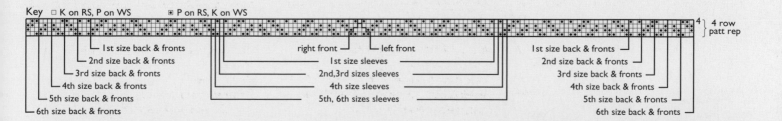

1st size back & fronts
2nd size back & fronts
3rd size back & fronts
4th size back & fronts
5th size back & fronts
6th size back & fronts

right front — └ left front
1st size sleeves
2nd, 3rd sizes sleeves
4th size sleeves
5th, 6th sizes sleeves

1st size back & fronts
2nd size back & fronts
3rd size back & fronts
4th size back & fronts
5th size back & fronts
6th size back & fronts

4 row patt rep

ROUND-NECK AND V-NECK TOPS

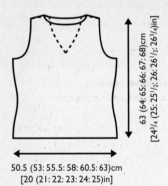

63 (64: 65: 66: 67: 68)cm [24¾ (25: 25½: 26: 26½: 26¾)in]

50.5 (53: 55.5: 58: 60.5: 63)cm [20 (21: 22: 23: 24: 25)in]

SIZES

1	2	3	4	5	6

TO FIT BUST

91	97	102	107	112	117	cm
36	38	40	42	44	46	in

YARNS

Rowan 4 ply Soft
ROUND-NECK TOP – light dusty
plum (378) – see page 105

7	7	8	8	8	9 x 50gm

V-NECK TOP – expresso (389) – see left

7	7	8	8	8	9 x 50gm

NEEDLES AND CROCHET HOOK

1 pair 2¾mm (no 12) (US 2) needles
1 pair 3¼mm (no 10) (US 3) needles
V-neck top only: 2.50mm (no 12) (US C-2)
crochet hook

TENSION

28 sts and 36 rows to 10cm/4in measured
over st st using 3¼mm (US 3) needles.

CROCHET ABBREVIATIONS

ss = slip stitch; **dc** = double crochet; **ch** =
chain; **tr** = treble.

ROUND-NECK TOP

BACK

Cast on 142 (150: 154: 162: 170: 178) sts using
2¾mm (US 2) needles.
Row 1 (RS): K2, *P2, K2, rep from * to end.
Row 2: P2, *K2, P2, rep from * to end.
These 2 rows form rib.
Work in rib for a further 4 rows, dec (dec: inc:
inc: dec: dec) 1 st at centre of last row and
ending with a WS row. 141 (149: 155: 163: 169:
177) sts.
Change to 3¼mm (US 3) needles.
Beg with a K row, work in st st as folls:
Work 36 rows, ending with a WS row.
Dec 1 st at each end of next and every foll
10th row to 133 (141: 147: 155: 161: 169) sts,
then on every foll 8th row until 129 (137: 143:
151: 157: 165) sts rem.
Work 11 rows, ending with a WS row.
Inc 1 st at each end of next and every foll 8th
row until there are 141 (149: 155: 163: 169:
177) sts.
Cont straight until back measures 42 (43: 43:
44: 44: 45)cm/16½ (16¾: 16¾: 17¼: 17½:
17¾)in, ending with a WS row.
Shape armholes
Cast off 7 (8: 8: 9: 9: 10) sts at beg of next 2
rows. 127 (133: 139: 145: 151: 157) sts.
Dec 1 st at each end of next 9 (9: 11: 11: 13:
13) rows, then on foll 7 (8: 8: 9: 9: 10) alt rows,
then on foll 4th row. 93 (97: 99: 103: 105:
109) sts.
Cont straight until armhole measures 21 (21:
22: 22: 23: 23)cm/8¼ (8¼: 8¾: 8¾: 9: 9)in,
ending with a WS row.
Shape shoulders and back neck
Cast off 6 (7: 7: 8: 8: 8) sts at beg of next 2
rows. 81 (83: 85: 87: 89: 93) sts.
Next row (RS): Cast off 6 (7: 7: 8: 8: 8) sts,
K until there are 11 (10: 11: 11: 11: 13) sts
on right needle and turn, leaving rem sts on
a holder.
Work each side of neck separately.
Cast off 4 sts at beg of next row.
Cast off rem 7 (6: 7: 7: 7: 9) sts.
With RS facing, rejoin yarn to rem sts, cast off
centre 47 (49: 49: 49: 51: 51) sts, K to end.
Complete to match first side, reversing
shapings.

FRONT

Work as given for back until 24 (26: 26: 26: 26:
26) rows less have been worked than on back
to start of shoulder shaping, ending with a
WS row.
Shape neck
Next row (RS): K 32 (34: 35: 37: 37: 39) sts
and turn, leaving rem sts on a holder.
Work each side of neck separately.
Dec 1 st at neck edge of next 9 rows, then on
foll 1 (2: 2: 2: 2: 2) alt rows, then on every foll
4th row until 19 (20: 21: 23: 23: 25) sts rem,

ending with a WS row.

Shape shoulder

Cast off 6 (7: 7: 8: 8: 8) sts at beg of next and foll alt row.

Work 1 row.

Cast off rem 7 (6: 7: 7: 7: 9) sts.

With RS facing, rejoin yarn to rem sts, cast off centre 29 (29: 29: 29: 31: 31) sts, K to end.

Complete to match first side, reversing shapings.

MAKING UP

PRESS as described on page 123.

Join right shoulder seam using backstitch, or mattress stitch if preferred.

Neckband

With RS facing and using 2¾mm (US 2) needles, pick up and knit 23 (24: 24: 24: 24: 24) sts down left side of neck, 29 (29: 29: 29: 31: 31) sts from front, 23 (24: 24: 24: 24: 24) sts up right side of neck, then 55 (57: 57: 57: 59: 59) sts from back. 130 (134: 134: 134: 138: 138) sts.

Beg with row 1, work in rib as given for back for 2 rows.

Cast off in rib (on WS).

Join left shoulder and neckband seam.

Armhole borders (both alike)

With RS facing and using 2¾mm (US 2) needles, pick up and knit 130 (134: 138: 142: 146: 150) sts all round armhole edge.

Beg with row 1, work in rib as given for back for 2 rows.

Cast off in rib (on WS).

See page 124 for finishing instructions.

V-NECK TOP

BACK

Cast on 141 (149: 155: 163: 169: 177) sts using 3¼mm (US 3) needles.

Beg with a K row, work in st st as folls:

Work 36 rows, ending with a WS row.

Dec 1 st at each end of next and every foll 10th row to 133 (141: 147: 155: 161: 169) sts,

then on every foll 8th row until 129 (137: 143: 151: 157: 165) sts rem.

Work 11 rows, ending with a WS row.

Inc 1 st at each end of next and every foll 8th row until there are 141 (149: 155: 163: 169: 177) sts.

Cont straight until back measures 41 (42: 42: 43: 43: 44)cm/16 (16¼: 16¼: 16¾: 17: 17¼)in, ending with a WS row.

Shape armholes

Cast off 7 (8: 8: 9: 9: 10) sts at beg of next 2 rows. 127 (133: 139: 145: 151: 157) sts.**

Dec 1 st at each end of next 9 (9: 11: 11: 13: 13) rows, then on foll 7 (8: 8: 9: 9: 10) alt rows, then on foll 4th row. 93 (97: 99: 103: 105: 109) sts.

Cont straight until armhole measures 21 (21: 22: 22: 23: 23)cm/8¼ (8¼: 8¾: 8¾: 9: 9)in, ending with a WS row.

Shape shoulders and back neck

Cast off 8 (8: 9: 9: 9: 10) sts at beg of next 2 rows. 77 (81: 81: 85: 87: 89) sts.

Next row (RS): Cast off 8 (8: 9: 9: 9: 10) sts, K until there are 12 (13: 12: 14: 14: 14) sts on right needle and turn, leaving rem sts on a holder.

Work each side of neck separately.

Cast off 4 sts at beg of next row.

Cast off rem 8 (9: 8: 10: 10: 10) sts.

With RS facing, rejoin yarn to rem sts, cast off centre 37 (39: 39: 39: 41: 41) sts, K to end.

Complete to match first side, reversing shapings.

FRONT

Work as given for back to **.

Dec 1 st at each end of next 8 rows, ending with a WS row. 111 (117: 123: 129: 135: 141) sts.

Divide for neck

Next row (RS): K2tog, K53 (56: 59: 62: 65: 68) and turn, leaving rem sts on a holder.

Work each side of neck separately.

Dec 0 (0: 1: 1: 1: 1) st at armhole edge of next row. 54 (57: 59: 62: 65: 68) sts.

Dec 1 st at armhole edge of next 1 (1: 1: 1: 3: 3) rows, then on foll 6 (7: 8: 9: 9: 10) alt rows,

then on foll 4th row **and at same time** dec 1 st at neck edge on next and every foll alt row. 37 (38: 38: 39: 39: 40) sts.

Dec 1 st at neck edge **only** on 2nd and foll 6 (7: 4: 3: 3: 2) alt rows, then on every foll 4th row until 24 (25: 26: 28: 28: 30) sts rem.

Cont straight until front matches back to start of shoulder shaping, ending with a WS row.

Shape shoulder

Cast off 8 (8: 9: 9: 9: 10) sts at beg of next and foll alt row.

Work 1 row.

Cast off rem 8 (9: 8: 10: 10: 10) sts.

With RS facing, rejoin yarn to rem sts, K2tog, K to last 2 sts, K2tog.

Complete to match first side, reversing shapings.

MAKING UP

PRESS as described on page 123.

Join shoulder seams using backstitch, or mattress stitch if preferred.

See page 124 for finishing instructions.

Edging

With 2.50mm (US C-2) crochet hook and RS facing, attach yarn to neck edge at one shoulder seam, 1ch (does NOT count as st), work one round of dc evenly around entire neck edge, working an even number of sts and ending with 1ss in first dc.

Next round (RS): 4ch (counts as 1tr and 1ch), (1tr, 1ch) 3 times into front loop only of dc at base of 4ch, (1ch, 1tr) 3 times into back loop only of same dc, 1tr into back loop of same dc, *miss 1dc, (1tr, 1ch) 4 times into front loop only of next dc, (1tr, 1ch) 3 times into back loop only of same st, 1tr into back loop of same dc, rep from * to last dc, miss last dc, 1ss in 3rd of 4ch at beg of round.

Fasten off.

In same way, work edging around armhole and lower edges.

CABLE-TRIM JACKET

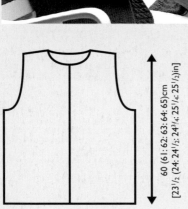

60 (61: 62: 63: 64: 65)cm
[23½ (24: 24½: 24¾: 25¼: 25½)in]

52.5 (55.5: 58: 60.5: 63.5: 66)cm
[20¾ (22: 23: 24: 25: 26)in]

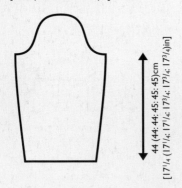

44 (44: 44: 45: 45: 45)cm
[17¼ (17¼: 17¼: 17¾: 17¾: 17¾)in]

SIZES

| 1 | 2 | 3 | 4 | 5 | 6 |

TO FIT BUST

| 91 | 97 | 102 | 107 | 112 | 117 | cm |
| 36 | 38 | 40 | 42 | 44 | 46 | in |

YARN

Jaeger Extra Fine Merino Chunky –
chocolate brown (022)

| 17 | 17 | 18 | 19 | 20 | 20 x 50gm |

NEEDLES

1 pair 5mm (no 6) (US 8) needles
1 pair 6mm (no 4) (US 10) needles
Cable needle

EXTRAS – 1 decorative pin or brooch

TENSION

15 sts and 20 rows to 10cm/4in measured
over st st using 6mm (US 10) needles.

SPECIAL ABBREVIATION

C4B = slip next 2 sts onto cable needle and
leave at back of work, K2, then K2 from
cable needle.

BACK

Cast on 79 (83: 87: 91: 95: 99) sts using 5mm
(US 8) needles.
Work in garter st for 6 rows, ending with a
WS row.
Change to 6mm (US 10) needles.
Row 7 (RS): Knit.
Row 8: K4, P to last 4 sts, K4.
Rep last 2 rows 7 times more.
Beg with a K row, cont in st st until back
measures 37 (38: 38: 39: 39: 40)cm/14½
(15: 15: 15¼: 15½: 15¾)in, ending with a
WS row.
Shape armholes
Cast off 4 (5: 5: 6: 6: 7) sts at beg of next 2
rows. 71 (73: 77: 79: 83: 85) sts.
Next row (RS): K2, K2tog, K to last 4 sts,
K2tog tbl, K2.

Next row: P2, P2tog tbl, P to last 4 sts,
P2tog, P2.
Working all decreases as set by last 2 rows,
dec 1 st at each end of next 1 (1: 3: 3: 5: 5)
rows, then on foll 3 alt rows, then on every
foll 4th row until 55 (57: 57: 59: 59: 61) sts rem.
Cont straight until armhole measures 23 (23:
24: 24: 25: 25)cm/9 (9: 9½: 9½: 9¾: 9¾)in,
ending with a WS row.
Shape shoulders and back neck
Cast off 5 (5: 5: 6: 5: 6) sts at beg of next 2
rows. 45 (47: 47: 47: 49: 49) sts.
Next row (RS): Cast off 5 (5: 5: 6: 5: 6) sts,
K until there are 10 (10: 10: 9: 10: 9) sts on
right needle and turn, leaving rem sts on a
holder.
Work each side of neck separately.
Cast off 4 sts at beg of next row.
Cast off rem 6 (6: 6: 5: 6: 5) sts.
With RS facing, rejoin yarn to rem sts, cast off
centre 15 (17: 17: 17: 19: 19) sts, K to end.
Complete to match first side, reversing
shapings.

LEFT FRONT

Cast on 40 (42: 44: 46: 48: 50) sts using 5mm
(US 8) needles.
Work in garter st for 6 rows, ending with a
WS row.
Change to 6mm (US 10) needles.
Row 7 (RS): Knit.
Row 8: P to last 4 sts, K4.
Rep last 2 rows 7 times more.
Beg with a K row, cont in st st until left front
matches back to beg of armhole shaping,
ending with a WS row.
Shape armhole
Cast off 4 (5: 5: 6: 6: 7) sts at beg of next row.
36 (37: 39: 40: 42: 43) sts.
Work 1 row.
Working all armhole decreases as set by back,
dec 1 st at armhole edge of next 3 (3: 5: 5: 7:
7) rows, then on foll 3 alt rows, then on
every foll 4th row until 28 (29: 29: 30: 30: 31)
sts rem.
Cont straight until 9 (11: 11: 11: 11: 11) rows

less have been worked than on back to start of shoulder shaping, ending with a RS row.

Shape neck

Cast off 6 (6: 6: 6: 7: 7) sts at beg of next row. 22 (23: 23: 24: 23: 24) sts.

Dec 1 st at neck edge of next 4 rows, then on foll 2 (3: 3: 3: 3: 3) alt rows, ending with a WS row. 16 (16: 16: 17: 16: 17) sts.

Shape shoulder

Cast off 5 (5: 5: 6: 5: 6) sts at beg of next and foll alt row.

Work 1 row.

Cast off rem 6 (6: 6: 5: 6: 5) sts.

RIGHT FRONT

Cast on 40 (42: 44: 46: 48: 50) sts using 5mm (US 8) needles.

Work in garter st for 6 rows, ending with a WS row.

Change to 6mm (US 10) needles.

Row 7 (RS): Knit.

Row 8: K4, P to end.

Rep last 2 rows 7 times more.

Complete to match left front, reversing shapings.

SLEEVES (both alike)

Cast on 43 (45: 45: 47: 49: 49) sts using 5mm (US 8) needles.

Work in garter st for 18 rows, ending with a WS row.

Change to 6mm (US 10) needles.

Beg with a K row, cont in st st, inc 1 st at each end of next and every foll 16th (16th: 12th: 12th: 12th: 10th) row to 53 (55: 53: 53: 55: 57) sts, then on every foll - (-: 14th: 14th: 14th: 12th) row until there are - (-: 57: 59: 61: 63) sts.

Cont straight until sleeve measures 44 (44: 44: 45: 45: 45)cm/17¼ (17¼: 17¼: 17¾: 17¾: 17¾)in, ending with a WS row.

Shape top

Cast off 4 (5: 5: 6: 6: 7) sts at beg of next 2 rows. 45 (45: 47: 47: 49: 49) sts.

Working all decreases as set by armholes, dec 1 st at each end of next 5 rows, then on foll 3

alt rows, then on every foll 4th row until 23 (23: 25: 25: 27: 27) sts rem.

Work 1 row, ending with a WS row.

Dec 1 st at each end of next and foll 0 (0: 1: 1: 2: 2) alt rows, then on foll 3 rows, ending with a WS row.

Cast off rem 15 sts.

MAKING UP

PRESS as described on page 123.

Join both shoulder seams using backstitch, or mattress stitch if preferred.

Collar

With RS facing and using 5mm (US 8) needles, starting and ending at front opening edges, pick up and knit 18 (20: 20: 20: 21: 21) sts up right side of neck, 23 (25: 25: 25: 27: 27) sts from back, then 18 (20: 20: 20: 21: 21) sts down left side of neck. 59 (65: 65: 65: 69: 69) sts.

Work in garter st until collar measures 12cm/4¾in, ending with RS of body facing for next row.

Cast off knitwise (on WS of collar).

Front bands (both alike)

With RS facing and using 5mm (US 8) needles, pick up and knit 86 sts along front opening edge, between cast-on edge and collar pick-up row.

**Row 1 (WS): P2, *K2, P2, rep from * to end.

Row 2: K2, *P2, inc once in each of next 2 sts, rep from * to last 4 sts, P2, K2. 126 sts.

Row 3: P2, K2, *P4, K2, rep from * to last 2 sts, P2.

Row 4: K2, P2, *C4B, P2, rep from * to last 2 sts, K2.

Row 5: As row 3.

Row 6: K2, P2, *K4, P2, rep from * to last 2 sts, K2.

Rows 7 to 10: As row 3 to 6.

Rows 11 and 12: As rows 3 and 4.

Cast off in patt (on WS).**

Collar bands (both alike)

With RS of collar facing (WS of body) and using 5mm (US 8) needles, pick up and knit 18

sts along front opening edge, between cast-off edge and collar pick-up row.

Work as given for front bands from ** to **, noting that there will be 24 sts after row 2. Join row-end edges of collar and front bands. See page 124 for finishing instructions, setting in sleeves using the set-in method and leaving side seams open for first 22 rows. Fasten front opening edges with decorative pin or brooch.

BOBBLE-TRIM SWEATER

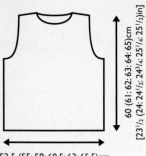

52.5 (55: 58: 60.5: 63: 65.5)cm
[20¾ (21¾: 23: 24: 25: 26)in]

60 (61: 62: 63: 64: 65)cm
[23½ (24: 24½: 24¾: 25¼: 25½)in]

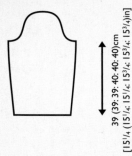

39 (39: 39: 40: 40: 40)cm
[15¼ (15¼: 15¼: 15¾: 15¾: 15¾)in]

SIZES

| 1 | 2 | 3 | 4 | 5 | 6 |

TO FIT BUST

| 91 | 97 | 102 | 107 | 112 | 117 | cm |
| 36 | 38 | 40 | 42 | 44 | 46 | in |

YARN

Rowan Cotton Glace – oyster (730)

| 14 | 14 | 15 | 16 | 16 | 17 x 50gm |

NEEDLES AND CROCHET HOOK

1 pair 2¾mm (no 12) (US 2) needles
1 pair 3¼mm (no 10) (US 3) needles
2.50mm (no 12) (US C-2) crochet hook

TENSION

23 sts and 32 rows to 10cm/4in measured over st st using 3¼mm (US 3) needles.

CROCHET ABBREVIATIONS

dc = double crochet; **ch** = chain; **dc2tog** = (insert hook into next st, yarn over hook and draw loop through) twice, yarn over hook and draw through all 3 loops on hook; **ss** = slip stitch.

BACK

Cast on 121 (127: 133: 139: 145: 151) sts using 2¾mm (US 2) needles.
Work in garter st for 6 rows, ending with a WS row.
Change to 3¼mm (US 3) needles.
Beg with a K row, cont in st st until back measures 37 (38: 38: 39: 39: 40)cm/14½ (15: 15: 157¼: 15½: 15¾)in, ending with a WS row.

Shape armholes

Cast off 6 (7: 7: 8: 8: 9) sts at beg of next 2 rows. 109 (113: 119: 123: 129: 133) sts.
Next row (RS): K3, K2tog, K to last 5 sts, K2tog tbl, K3.
Next row: P3, P2tog tbl, P to last 5 sts, P2tog, P3.
Working all armhole decreases as set by last 2 rows, dec 1 st at each end of next 3 (3: 5: 5: 7: 7) rows, then on foll 4 (5: 5: 6: 6: 7) alt rows,

then on every foll 4th row until 87 (89: 91: 93: 95: 97) sts rem.
Cont straight until armhole measures 23 (23: 24: 24: 25: 25)cm/9 (9: 9½: 9½: 9¾: 9¾)in, ending with a WS row.

Shape shoulders and back neck

Cast off 5 (5: 5: 6: 6: 6) sts at beg of next 2 rows. 77 (79: 81: 81: 83: 85) sts.
Next row (RS): Cast off 5 (5: 5: 6: 6: 6) sts, K until there are 9 (9: 10: 9: 9: 10) sts on right needle and turn, leaving rem sts on a holder.
Work each side of neck separately.
Cast off 4 sts at beg of next row.
Cast off rem 5 (5: 6: 5: 5: 6) sts.
With RS facing, rejoin yarn to rem sts, cast off centre 49 (51: 51: 51: 53: 53) sts, K to end.
Complete to match first side, reversing shapings.

FRONT

Work as given for back until 16 (18: 18: 18: 18: 18) rows less have been worked than on back to start of shoulder shaping, ending with a WS row.

Shape neck

Next row (RS): K29 (30: 31: 32: 32: 33) and turn, leaving rem sts on a holder.
Work each side of neck separately.
Cast off 5 sts at beg of next row. 24 (25: 26: 27: 27: 28) sts.
Dec 1 st at neck edge of next 4 rows, then on foll 5 (6: 6: 6: 6: 6) alt rows, ending with a WS row. 15 (15: 16: 17: 17: 18) sts.

Shape shoulder

Cast off 5 (5: 5: 6: 6: 6) sts at beg of next and foll alt row.
Work 1 row.
Cast off rem 5 (5: 6: 5: 5: 6) sts.
With RS facing, rejoin yarn to rem sts, cast off centre 29 (29: 29: 29: 31: 31) sts, K to end.
Complete to match first side, reversing shapings.

SLEEVES (both alike)

Cast on 67 (69: 69: 71: 73: 73) sts using 2¾mm (US 2) needles.

Work in garter st for 6 rows, ending with a WS row.

Change to 3¼mm (US 3) needles.

Beg with a K row, cont in st st, shaping sides by inc 1 st at each end of 5th and every foll 12th (12th: 10th: 10th: 10th: 10th) row to 83 (85: 81: 79: 81: 93) sts, then on every foll 14th (14th: 12th: 12th: 12th: 12th) row until there are 85 (87: 89: 91: 93: 95) sts.

Cont straight until sleeve measures 39 (39: 39: 40: 40: 40)cm/15¼ (15¼: 15¼: 15¾: 15¾: 15¾)in, ending with a WS row.

Shape top

Cast off 6 (7: 7: 8: 8: 9) sts at beg of next 2 rows. 73 (73: 75: 75: 77: 77) sts.

Working all decreases as set by back and front armholes, dec 1 st at each end of next 7 rows, then on foll 5 alt rows, then on every foll 4th row until 39 (39: 41: 41: 43: 43) sts rem.

Work 1 row, ending with a WS row.

Dec 1 st at each end of next and every foll alt row to 33 sts, then on foll 5 rows, ending with a WS row.

Cast off rem 23 sts.

MAKING UP

PRESS as described on page 123.

Join right shoulder seam using backstitch.

Neckband

With RS facing and using 2¾mm (US 2) needles, pick up and knit 20 (22: 22: 22: 22: 22) sts down left side of neck, 29 (29: 29: 29: 31: 31) sts from front, 20 (22: 22: 22: 22: 22) sts up right side of neck, then 57 (59: 59: 59: 61: 61) sts from back. 126 (132: 132: 132: 136: 136) sts.

Work in garter st for 2 rows, ending with a RS row.

Cast off knitwise (on WS).

See page 124 for finishing instructions, setting in sleeves using the set-in method.

Bobbles

With 2.50mm (US C-2) crochet hook, make a slip loop.

Round 1 (RS): 8dc in centre of slip loop, 1ss in first dc.

Pull firmly on loose end of slip loop to close base of bobble.

Round 2: 1ch (does NOT count as st), 2dc in each dc to end, 1ss in first dc. 16 sts.

Round 3: 1ch (does NOT count as st), 1dc in each dc to end, 1ss in first dc.

Round 4: 1ch (does NOT count as st), (dc2tog over next 2dc) 8 times, 1ss in first dc2tog. 8 sts.

Fasten off, leaving a fairly long end. Insert a little toy filling into bobble and run a gathering thread around top of last row. Pull up tight and fasten off securely.

Make 62 (64: 66: 70: 72: 74) bobbles in total.

Edging

**With 2.50mm (US C-2) crochet hook and RS facing, rejoin yarn at base of one side seam and cont as folls:

Round 1 (RS): 1ch (does NOT count as st), 1dc in first cast-on st, *10ch, 1dc in top of bobble, 10ch, miss 11 cast-on sts, 1dc in next st, rep from * to end, replacing dc at end of last rep with 1ss in first dc.

Fasten off.

Beg at other side seam, rep from ** once more, working dc into sts midway between sts used for first round.

Work edging around cast-on edge of sleeves in same way.

TASSEL-TRIM SWEATER

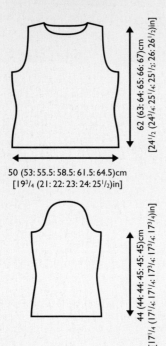

62 (63: 64: 65: 66: 67)cm
[24½ (24¾: 25¼: 25½: 26: 26½)in]

50 (53: 55.5: 58.5: 61.5: 64.5)cm
[19¾ (21: 22: 23: 24: 25½)in]

44 (44: 44: 45: 45: 45)cm
[17¼ (17¼: 17¼: 17¾: 17¾: 17¾)in]

SIZES

1	2	3	4	5	6

TO FIT BUST

91	97	102	107	112	117	cm
36	38	40	42	44	46	in

YARN

Rowan Calmer – cream (460)

8	8	9	9	10	10 x 50gm

NEEDLES

1 pair 4mm (no 8) (US 6) needles
1 pair 5mm (no 6) (US 8) needles
2 double-pointed 4mm (no 8) (US 6) needles

TENSION

21 sts and 30 rows to 10cm/4in measured over st st using 5mm (US 8) needles.

SPECIAL ABBREVIATION

tassel 3 = Holding WS of tassel against RS of main section, K tog first st of tassel with next st of main section, K tog next 2 sts of tassel with next 2 sts of main section in same way.

TASSELS

Cast on 3 sts using double-pointed 4mm (US 6) needles.
Row 1 (RS): K3, *without turning slip these 3 sts to opposite end of needle and bring yarn to opposite end of work pulling it quite tightly across WS of work, K these 3 sts again, rep from * until tassel is 5cm/2in long.
Break yarn and leave sts on a holder.
Make required number of tassels in this way – you will need 36 (44: 44: 44: 52: 52) for back, same number for front, and 28 for each sleeve.

BACK

Cast on 105 (111: 117: 123: 129: 135) sts using 4mm (US 6) needles. Work in garter st for 4 rows, ending with a WS row.
Row 5 (RS): K11 (4: 7: 10: 3: 6), tassel 3, *K7, tassel 3, rep from * to last 11 (4: 7: 10: 3: 6) sts, K to end.

Row 6: Knit.
Change to 5mm (US 8) needles.
Beg with a K row, work in st st for 8 rows, ending with a WS row.
Last 10 rows form tassel patt.
Using 5mm (US 8) needles throughout, work a further 22 rows in tassel patt, ending with a WS row. (4 rows of tassels completed.)
Beg with a K row, cont in st st, dec 1 st at each end of next and every foll 12th row until 97 (103: 109: 115: 121: 127) sts rem.
Work 9 rows, ending with a WS row.
Inc 1 st at each end of next and every foll 10th row until there are 105 (111: 117: 123: 129: 135) sts.
Cont straight until back measures 39 (40: 40: 41: 41: 42)cm/15½ (15¾: 15¾: 16: 16¼: 16¾)in, ending with a WS row.

Shape armholes

Cast off 5 (6: 6: 7: 7: 8) sts at beg of next 2 rows. 95 (99: 105: 109: 115: 119) sts.
Dec 1 st at each end of next 5 (5: 7: 7: 9: 9) rows, then on foll 2 (3: 3: 4: 4: 5) alt rows, then on every foll 4th row until 77 (79: 81: 83: 85: 87) sts rem.
Cont straight until armhole measures 23 (23: 24: 24: 25: 25)cm/9 (9: 9½: 9½: 9¾: 9¾)in, ending with a WS row.

Shape shoulders and back neck

Cast off 5 (5: 6: 6: 6: 6) sts at beg of next 2 rows. 67 (69: 69: 71: 73: 75) sts.
Next row (RS): Cast off 5 (5: 6: 6: 6: 6) sts, K until there are 10 (10: 9: 10: 10: 11) sts on right needle and turn, leaving rem sts on a holder.
Work each side of neck separately.
Cast off 4 sts at beg of next row.
Cast off rem 6 (6: 5: 6: 6: 7) sts.
With RS facing, rejoin yarn to rem sts, cast off centre 37 (39: 39: 39: 41: 41) sts, K to end.
Complete to match first side, reversing shapings.

FRONT

Work as given for back until 12 (14: 14: 14: 14: 14) rows less have been worked than on back to start of shoulder shaping, ending with a WS row.

Shape neck

Next row (RS): K28 (29: 30: 31: 31: 32) and turn, leaving rem sts on a holder.

Work each side of neck separately.

Cast off 5 sts at beg of next row. 23 (24: 25: 26: 26: 27) sts.

Dec 1 st at neck edge of next 5 rows, then on foll 2 (3: 3: 3: 3: 3) alt rows. 16 (16: 17: 18: 18: 19) sts.

Work 1 row, ending with a WS row.

Shape shoulder

Cast off 5 (5: 6: 6: 6: 6) sts at beg of next and foll alt row.

Work 1 row.

Cast off rem 6 (6: 5: 6: 6: 7) sts.

With RS facing, rejoin yarn to rem sts, cast off centre 21 (21: 21: 21: 23: 23) sts, K to end.

Complete to match first side, reversing shapings.

SLEEVES (both alike)

Cast on 79 (81: 81: 83: 85: 85) sts using 4mm (US 6) needles.

Work in garter st for 4 rows, ending with a WS row.

Row 5 (RS): K8 (9: 9: 10: 11: 11), tassel 3, *K7, tassel 3, rep from * to last 8 (9: 9: 10: 11: 11) sts, K to end.

Row 6: Knit.

Change to 5mm (US 8) needles.

Beg with a K row, work in st st for 8 rows, dec 1 st at each end of 7th of these rows and ending with a WS row. 77 (79: 79: 81: 83: 83) sts.

Last 10 rows form tassel patt and start sleeve shaping.

Using 5mm (US 8) needles throughout, work a further 22 rows in tassel patt **and at same time** dec 1 st at each end of 5th and every foll 6th row, ending with a WS row. (4 rows of tassels completed.) 71 (73: 73: 75: 77: 77) sts.

Beg with a K row, cont in st st, dec 1 st at each end of next and every foll 6th row to 65 (67: 67: 69: 71: 71) sts, then on every foll 8th

row until 61 (63: 63: 65: 67: 67) sts rem.

Work 11 rows, ending with a WS row.

Inc 1 st at each end of next and every foll 6th (6th: 4th: 4th: 4th: 4th) row to 77 (79: 71: 71: 73: 79) sts, then on every foll - (-: 6th: 6th: 6th: 6th) row until there are - (-: 81: 83: 85: 87) sts.

Cont straight until sleeve measures 44 (44: 44: 45: 45: 45)cm/17¼ (17¼: 17¼: 17¾: 17¾: 17¾)in, ending with a WS row.

Shape top

Keeping patt correct, cast off 5 (6: 6: 7: 7: 8) sts at beg of next 2 rows. 67 (67: 69: 69: 71: 71) sts.

Dec 1 st at each end of next 7 rows, then on foll 3 alt rows, then on every foll 4th row until 39 (39: 41: 41: 43: 43) sts rem.

Work 1 row, ending with a WS row.

Dec 1 st at each end of next and every foll alt row to 27 sts, then on foll 3 rows, ending with a WS row.

Cast off rem 21 sts.

MAKING UP

PRESS as described on page 123.

Join right shoulder seam using backstitch, or mattress stitch if preferred.

Neckband

With RS facing and using 4mm (US 6) needles, pick up and knit 18 (20: 20: 20: 20: 20) sts down left side of neck, 21 (21: 21: 21: 23: 23) sts from front, 18 (20: 20: 20: 20: 20) sts up right side of neck, then 45 (47: 47: 47: 49: 49) sts from back. 102 (108: 108: 108: 112: 112) sts.

Work in garter st for 2 rows.

Cast off knitwise (on WS).

See page 124 for finishing instructions, setting in sleeves using the set-in method.

CABLE-TRIM SWEATER

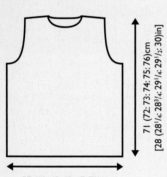

71 (72: 73: 74: 75: 76)cm
[28 (28¹/₄: 28³/₄: 29¹/₄: 29¹/₂: 30)in]

57 (60: 62: 65: 67: 70)cm
[22¹/₂ (23¹/₂: 24¹/₄: 25¹/₂: 26¹/₂: 27¹/₂)in]

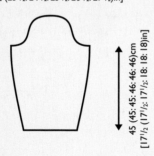

45 (45: 45: 46: 46: 46)cm
[17¹/₂ (17¹/₂: 17¹/₂: 18: 18: 18)in]

SIZES

1	2	3	4	5	6

TO FIT BUST

91	97	102	107	112	117	cm
36	38	40	42	44	46	in

YARN

Rowan Denim – ecru (324)

16	17	18	19	20	21 x 50gm

NEEDLES

1 pair 3¼mm (no 10) (US 3) needles
1 pair 4mm (no 8) (US 6) needles
Cable needle

TENSION

Before washing: 20 sts and 28 rows to 10cm/4in measured over st st using 4mm (US 6) needles.

Tension note: Denim will shrink in length when washed for the first time. Allowances have been made in the pattern for shrinkage (see size diagram for after washing measurements).

SPECIAL ABBREVIATIONS

CB4 = slip next 2 sts onto cable needle and leave at back of work, K2, then K2 from cable needle.
C4F = slip next 2 sts onto cable needle and leave at front of work, K2, then K2 from cable needle.

BACK

Cast on 144 (150: 158: 164: 172: 178) sts using 3¼mm (US 3) needles.
Row 1 (RS): (P2, K2) 3 (2: 3: 2: 3: 2) times, *P2, K4, (P2, K2) twice, rep from * to last 6 (2: 6: 2: 6: 2) sts, P2, (K2, P2) 1 (0: 1: 0: 1: 0) times.
Row 2 and every foll alt row: (K2, P2) 3 (2: 3: 2: 3: 2) times, *K2, P4, (K2, P2) twice, rep from * to last 6 (2: 6: 2: 6: 2) sts, K2, (P2, K2) 1 (0: 1: 0: 1: 0) times.
Row 3: (P2, K2) 3 (2: 3: 2: 3: 2) times, *P2,

C4B, (P2, K2) twice, rep from * to last 6 (2: 6: 2: 6: 2) sts, P2, (K2, P2) 1 (0: 1: 0: 1: 0) times.
Row 5: As row 1.
Row 7: (P2, K2) 3 (2: 3: 2: 3: 2) times, *P2, C4F, (P2, K2) twice, rep from * to last 6 (2: 6: 2: 6: 2) sts, P2, (K2, P2) 1 (0: 1: 0: 1: 0) times.
Row 8: As row 2.
These 8 rows form fancy rib.
Cont in fancy rib for a further 31 rows, ending with a RS row.
Row 40 (dec) (WS): Rib 4 (0: 2: 5: 0: 3), *rib 1 (2: 1: 1: 1: 1), work 2 tog, rib 3, work 2 tog, rib 1, rep from * to last 5 (0: 3: 6: 1: 4) sts, rib 5 (0: 3: 6: 1: 4). 114 (120: 124: 130: 134: 140) sts.
Change to 4mm (US 6) needles.
Beg with a K row, cont in st st until back measures 56 (57: 57: 58.5: 58.5: 59.5)cm/22 (22¼: 22½: 23: 23: 23¼)in, ending with a WS row.
Shape armholes
Cast off 6 (7: 7: 8: 8: 9) sts at beg of next 2 rows. 102 (106: 110: 114: 118: 122) sts.
Dec 1 st at each end of next 5 (5: 7: 7: 9: 9) rows, then on foll 5 (6: 5: 6: 5: 6) alt rows, then on every foll 4th row until 78 (80: 82: 84: 86: 88) sts rem.
Cont straight until armhole measures 27 (27: 28: 28: 29: 29)cm/10¾ (10¾: 11: 11: 11½: 11½)in, ending with a WS row.
Shape shoulders and back neck
Cast off 7 (7: 8: 8: 8: 8) sts at beg of next 2 rows. 64 (66: 66: 68: 70: 72) sts.
Next row (RS): Cast off 7 (7: 8: 8: 8: 8) sts, K until there are 12 (12: 11: 12: 12: 13) sts on right needle and turn, leaving rem sts on a holder.
Work each side of neck separately.
Cast off 4 sts at beg of next row.
Cast off rem 8 (8: 7: 8: 8: 9) sts.
With RS facing, rejoin yarn to rem sts, cast off centre 26 (28: 28: 28: 30: 30) sts, K to end.
Complete to match first side, reversing shapings.

FRONT

Work as given for back until 16 (18: 18: 18: 18: 18) rows less have been worked than on back to start of shoulder shaping, ending with a WS row.

Shape neck

Next row (RS): K31 (32: 33: 34: 34: 35) and turn, leaving rem sts on a holder.

Work each side of neck separately.

Dec 1 st at neck edge of next 5 rows, then on foll 3 (4: 4: 4: 4: 4) alt rows, then on foll 4th row, ending with a WS row. 22 (22: 23: 24: 24: 25) sts.

Shape shoulder

Cast off 7 (7: 8: 8: 8: 8) sts at beg of next and foll alt row.

Work 1 row.

Cast off rem 8 (8: 7: 8: 8: 9) sts.

With RS facing, rejoin yarn to rem sts, cast off centre 16 (16: 16: 16: 18: 18) sts, K to end.

Complete to match first side, reversing shapings.

SLEEVES (both alike)

Cast on 58 (60: 60: 62: 64: 64) sts using 3¼mm (US 3) needles.

Row 1 (RS): K0 (0: 0: 1: 2: 2), P1 (2: 2: 2: 2: 2), (K2, P2) 3 times, *K4, (P2, K2) twice, P2, rep from * to last 3 (4: 4: 5: 6: 6) sts, K2, P1 (2: 2: 2: 2: 2), K0 (0: 0: 1: 2: 2).

Row 2 and every foll alt row: P0 (0: 0: 1: 2: 2), K1 (2: 2: 2: 2: 2), (P2, K2) 3 times, *P4, (K2, P2) twice, K2, rep from * to last 3 (4: 4: 5: 6: 6) sts, P2, K1 (2: 2: 2: 2: 2), P0 (0: 0: 1: 2: 2).

Row 3: K0 (0: 0: 1: 2: 2), P1 (2: 2: 2: 2: 2), (K2, P2) 3 times, *C4B, (P2, K2) twice, P2, rep from * to last 3 (4: 4: 5: 6: 6) sts, K2, P1 (2: 2: 2: 2: 2), K0 (0: 0: 1: 2: 2).

Row 5: As row 1.

Row 7: K0 (0: 0: 1: 2: 2), P1 (2: 2: 2: 2: 2), (K2, P2) 3 times, *C4F, (P2, K2) twice, P2, rep from * to last 3 (4: 4: 5: 6: 6) sts, K2, P1 (2: 2: 2: 2: 2), K0 (0: 0: 1: 2: 2).

Row 8: As row 2.

These 8 rows form fancy rib.

Cont in fancy rib for a further 15 rows, ending with a RS row.

Row 24 (dec) (WS): Rib 1 (2: 2: 3: 4: 4), work 2 tog, *rib 3, work 2 tog, rep from * to

last 0 (1: 1: 2: 3: 3) sts, rib 0 (1: 1: 2: 3: 3). 46 (48: 48: 50: 52: 52) sts.

Change to 4mm (US 6) needles.

Beg with a K row, cont in st st, inc 1 st at each end of next and every foll 6th row to 58 (60: 68: 68: 70: 78) sts, then on every foll 8th row until there are 78 (80: 82: 84: 86: 88) sts.

Cont straight until sleeve measures 52.5 (52.5: 52.5: 53.5: 53.5: 53.5)cm/20¾ (20¾: 20¾: 21: 21: 21)in, ending with a WS row.

Shape top

Cast off 6 (7: 7: 8: 8: 9) sts at beg of next 2 rows. 66 (66: 68: 68: 70: 70) sts.

Dec 1 st at each end of next 7 rows, then on foll 5 alt rows, then on every foll 4th row until 30 (30: 32: 32: 34: 34) sts rem.

Work 1 row, ending with a WS row.

Dec 1 st at each end of next and every foll alt row to 26 sts, then on foll 3 rows, ending with a WS row.

Cast off rem 20 sts.

MAKING UP

Do NOT press.

Join right shoulder seam using backstitch.

Collar

With RS facing and using 3¼mm (US 3) needles, pick up and knit 24 (24: 24: 24: 27: 27) sts down left side of neck, 16 (16: 16: 16: 20: 20) sts from front, 24 (24: 24: 24: 27: 27) sts up right side of neck, then 36 (36: 36: 36: 40: 40) sts from back. 100 (100: 100: 100: 114: 114) sts.

Row 1 (RS of collar, WS of body): P2, *K2, P2, K4, P2, K2, P2, rep from * to end.

Row 2 and every foll alt row: K2, *P2, K2, P4, K2, P2, K2, rep from * to end.

Row 3: P2, *K2, P2, C4B, P2, K2, P2, rep from * to end.

Row 5: As row 1.

Row 7: P2, *K2, P2, C4F, P2, K2, P2, rep from * to end.

Row 8: As row 2.

These 8 rows form fancy rib.

Cont in fancy rib until collar measures 7cm/2¾in.

Change to 4mm (US 6) needles.

Cont in fancy rib until collar measures 15cm/6in.

Cast off in rib.

Machine wash all pieces before completing sewing together.

See page 124 for finishing instructions, setting in sleeves using the set-in method.

MOTIF BAG

YARNS

Jaeger Extra Fine Merino DK

A	charcoal (959)	1 x 50gm
B	oatmeal (936)	1 x 50gm
C	camel (938)	1 x 50gm
D	grey tweed (978)	1 x 50gm

CROCHET HOOK

3.50mm (no 9) (US E-4) crochet hook

EXTRAS – 30cm/12in by 60cm/24in piece of fabric for lining

TENSION

Basic motif measures 8cm/3⅛in square using 3.50mm (US E-4) hook.

FINISHED SIZE

Completed bag measures 24cm/9½in wide and 26cm/10¼in deep.

CROCHET ABBREVIATIONS

ch = chain; **ss** = slip stitch; **dc** = double crochet; **tr** = treble; **sp(s)** = space(es); **dtr3tog** = *(yoh) twice and insert hook as indicated, yoh and draw loop through, (yoh and draw through 2 loops) twice, rep from * twice more, yoh and draw through all 4 loops on hook; **dtr4tog** = *(yoh) twice and insert

hook as indicated, yoh and draw loop through, (yoh and draw through 2 loops) twice, rep from * 3 times more, yoh and draw through all 5 loops on hook; **yoh** = yarn over hook.

BASIC MOTIF

Make 6ch using 3.50mm (US E-4) hook and join with a ss in first ch to form a ring.
Round 1 (WS): 4ch (counts as 1tr and 1ch), (1tr in ring, 1ch) 7 times, 1ss in 3rd of 4ch at beg of round.
Round 2: 1ss in first ch sp, 4ch (does NOT count as st), dtr3tog in same ch sp, (4ch, dtr4tog in next ch sp) 7 times, 4ch, 1ss in top of dtr3tog at beg of round.
Round 3: 1ch (does NOT count as st), 1dc in same place as ss at end of previous round, *4ch, 1tr in next ch sp, 4ch, 1dc in next dtr4tog, 4ch, miss 4ch**, 1dc in next dtr4tog, rep from * to end, ending last rep at **, 1ss in first dc.
Round 4: 1ch (does NOT count as st), 1dc in same place as ss at end of previous round, *4dc in next ch sp, 3dc in next tr**, (4dc in next ch sp, 1dc in next dc) twice, rep from * to end, ending last rep at **, 4dc in next ch sp, 1dc in next dc, 4dc in next ch sp, 1ss in first dc.
Fasten off.
Basic motif is a square. In each corner there are 3dc and between these corner dc there are a further 14dc.

BAG

Make 18 basic motifs in total – 6 in yarn A, 3 in yarn B, 4 in yarn C and 5 in yarn D.
Foll diagram, join motifs to form a strip 6 motifs wide and 3 motifs deep by sewing (or crocheting) motifs together along side of central 10dc along joining edges. Join ends of strip to form a tube in same way, then join base seam in same way.

Edging

With RS facing, using 3.50mm (US E-4) hook and yarn A, join yarn along one edge of one of top opening edge motifs, joining yarn to 3rd dc

after the corner dc, and cont as folls:
Edging round (RS): 1ch (does NOT count as st), 1dc in same place as where yarn was joined, 1dc in each of next 9dc of same motif, *5ch**, miss 3 corner dc and foll 2dc of next motif, 1dc in each of next 10dc, rep from * to end, ending last rep at **, 1ss in first dc. 90 sts.
Next round: 1ch (does NOT count as st), 1dc in each dc and 5dc in each ch sp to end, 1ss in first dc.
Next round: 1ch (does NOT count as st), 1dc in each dc to end, 1ss in first dc.
Rep last round once more.
Fasten off.

HANDLES (make 2)

Make 65ch using 3.50mm (US E-4) hook and yarn A.
Row 1: 1dc in 2nd ch from hook, 1dc in each dc to end, turn. 64 sts.
Row 2: 1ch (does NOT count as st), 1dc in each dc to end, turn.
Rep row 2 twice more.
Fasten off.

MAKING UP

PRESS as described on page 123.
Attach ends of handles inside upper opening edge of bag, positioning ends of handles 10cm/4in apart.
Cut 2 pieces of fabric same size as finished bag, adding seam allowance along all edges. Join lining pieces along side and lower edges. Fold seam allowance to WS around upper edge. Slip lining inside bag and slip stitch in place around upper edge.

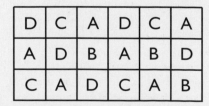

D	C	A	D	C	A
A	D	B	A	B	D
C	A	D	C	A	B

MOTIF SCARF

YARNS

Jaeger Extra Fine Merino DK

A charcoal (959)   2 x 50gm
B oatmeal (936)   2 x 50gm
C camel (938)   2 x 50gm
D grey tweed (978)   2 x 50gm

CROCHET HOOK

3.50mm (no 9) (US E-4) crochet hook

TENSION

Basic motif measures 8cm/3⅛in square using 3.50mm (US E-4) hook.

FINISHED SIZE

Completed scarf measures 25cm/10in wide and 177cm/69½in long.

CROCHET ABBREVIATIONS

Abbreviations as for motif bag (see page 88).

BASIC MOTIF

Make as for basic motif for motif bag (see page 88).

SCARF

Make 66 basic motifs in total – 15 in yarn A, 17 in yarn B, 17 in yarn C and 17 in yarn D. Foll diagram, join motifs to form a strip 22

motifs long and 3 motifs wide by sewing (or crocheting) motifs together along side of central 10dc along joining edges.

Edging

With RS facing, using 3.50mm (US E-4) hook and yarn A, join yarn along one long edge of joined motifs, joining yarn to 3rd dc after the corner dc, and cont as folls:

Edging round (RS): 1ch (does NOT count as st), 1dc in same place as where yarn was joined, 1dc in each of next 9dc of same motif, *(5ch**, miss 3 corner dc and foll 2dc of next motif, 1dc in each of next 10dc) to end motif, 5ch, miss 3 corner dc and foll 2dc of end motif, 1dc in each of next 13dc, 2dc in centre dc of corner group of 3dc, 1dc in each of next 13dc, rep from * to end, ending last rep at **, 1ss in first dc.

Next round: 1ch (does NOT count as st), 1dc in each dc and 5dc in each ch sp to end, 1ss in first dc.

Fasten off.

MAKING UP

PRESS as described on page 123.

C	A	B
A	B	D
D	C	A
B	D	C
C	A	B
B	C	D
D	B	A
A	D	C
C	B	A
A	D	C
B	C	D
A	D	B
B	C	A
A	B	D
B	C	A
C	D	B
D	A	C
C	B	D
A	D	C
D	C	B
B	A	D
D	C	B

BOBBLE-TRIM SCARF

YARN
Rowan Cotton Glace – oyster (730)
5 x 50gm

NEEDLES AND CROCHET HOOK
1 pair 2¾mm (no 12) (US 2) needles
2.50mm (no 12) (US C-2) crochet hook

EXTRAS – washable toy filling

TENSION
25 sts and 42 rows to 10cm/4in measured
over moss stitch using 2¾mm (US 2) needles.

FINISHED SIZE
Completed scarf measures 17cm/6½in wide
and 160cm/63in long, excluding bobble trim.

CROCHET ABBREVIATIONS
dc = double crochet; **ch**= chain; **dc2tog** =
(insert hook into next st, yarn over hook and
draw loop through) twice, yarn over hook
and draw through all 3 loops on hook; **ss** =
slip stitch.

SCARF
Cast on 43 sts using 2¾mm (US 2) needles.
Row 1 (RS): K1, *P1, K1, rep from * to end.
Row 2: As row 1.

These 2 rows form moss st.
Cont in moss st until scarf measures
160cm/63in, ending with a WS row.
Cast off in moss st.

MAKING UP
PRESS as described on page 123.
Bobbles (make 10)
With 2.50mm (US C-2) crochet hook, make a
slip loop.
Round 1 (RS): 8dc in centre of slip loop, 1ss
in first dc.
Pull firmly on loose end of slip loop to close
base of bobble.
Round 2: 1ch (does NOT count as st), 2dc in
each dc to end, 1ss in first dc. 16 sts.
Round 3: 1ch (does NOT count as st), 1dc in
each dc to end, 1ss in first dc.
Round 4: 1ch (does NOT count as st),
(dc2tog over next 2dc) 8 times, 1ss in first
dc2tog. 8 sts.
Fasten off, leaving a fairly long end. Insert a
little toy filling into bobble and run a gathering
thread around top of last row. Pull up tight and
fasten off securely.
Edging
With 2.50mm (US C-2) crochet hook and RS
facing, rejoin yarn at beg of cast-off edge and
cont as folls:
Row 1 (RS): 1ch (does NOT count as st),
1dc in first cast-off st, 9ch, 1dc in top of
bobble, 9ch, miss 12 cast-off sts, 1dc in each of
next 2 sts, 9ch, 1dc in top of next bobble, 9ch,
miss 13 cast-off sts, 1dc in each of next 2 sts,
9ch, 1dc in top of next bobble, 9ch, miss 12
cast-off sts, 1dc in last st, turn, 1 ss in each of
next 6 cast-off sts, 1ch, 1dc in same st as last
ss, (9ch, 1dc in top of next bobble, 9ch, miss 14
cast-off sts, 1dc in next st) twice.
Fasten off.
Work edging across cast-on edge in same way.

CABLED SCARF

These 12 rows form patt.
Cont in patt until scarf measures approx
202cm/79½in, ending after patt row 4.
Cast off in patt.

MAKING UP
PRESS as described on page 123.
Cut 35cm/13¾in lengths of yarn and knot
groups of 4 of these lengths through every
3rd st along cast-on and cast-off edges to
form fringe.

YARN
Rowan Calmer – ecru (461)
4 x 50gm

NEEDLES
1 pair 5mm (no 6) (US 8) needles
Cable needle

TENSION
21 sts and 30 rows to 10cm/4in measured
over st st using 5mm (US 8) needles.

FINISHED SIZE
Completed scarf measures 15cm/6in wide and
202cm/79½in long, excluding fringe.

SPECIAL ABBREVIATION
C12B = slip next 6 sts onto cable needle
and leave at back of work, K6, then K6 from
cable needle.

SCARF
Cast on 57 sts using 5mm (US 8) needles.
Cont in patt as folls:
Row 1 (RS): K12, (P3, K12) 3 times.
Row 2: P12, (K1, yfwd, K2tog, P12) 3 times.
Row 3: C12B, (P3, C12B) 3 times.
Row 4: As row 2.
Rows 5 to 12: As rows 1 and 2, 4 times.

GARTER-RIB SWEATER

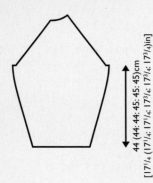

56 (59.5: 61.5: 65: 67: 70.5)cm
[22 (23¹/₂: 24¹/₄: 25¹/₂: 26¹/₂: 27³/₄)in]

69 (70: 71: 72: 73: 73)cm
[27¹/₄ (27¹/₂: 28: 28¹/₄: 28³/₄: 28³/₄)in]

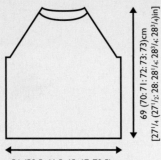

44 (44: 44: 45: 45: 45)cm
[17¹/₄ (17¹/₄: 17¹/₄: 17³/₄: 17³/₄: 17³/₄)in]

SIZES

| 1 | 2 | 3 | 4 | 5 | 6 | |

TO FIT BUST

| 91 | 97 | 102 | 107 | 112 | 117 | cm |
| 36 | 38 | 40 | 42 | 44 | 46 | in |

YARN

Rowan All Seasons Cotton – mocha (212)

| 16 | 16 | 17 | 18 | 18 | 19 x 50gm |

NEEDLES

1 pair 4mm (no 8) (US 6) needles
1 pair 4¹/₂mm (no 7) (US 7) needles

TENSION

18 sts and 25 rows to 10cm/4in measured over st st using 4¹/₂mm (US 7) needles.

BACK

Cast on 101 (107: 111: 117: 121: 127) sts using 4mm (US 6) needles.
Row 1 (WS): Purl.
Row 2: P2 (0: 2: 0: 2: 0), *K2, P3, rep from * to last 4 (2: 4: 2: 4: 2) sts, K2, P2 (0: 2: 0: 2: 0).
These 2 rows form patt.
Work in patt for a further 3 rows, ending with a WS row.
Change to 4¹/₂mm (US 7) needles.
Cont in patt until back measures 43cm/17in, ending with a WS row.
Shape raglan armholes
Keeping patt correct, cast off 4 sts at beg of next 2 rows. 93 (99: 103: 109: 113: 119) sts.
1st and 2nd sizes only
Dec 1 st at each end of next and foll 4th row. 87 (95: -: -: -: -) sts.
Work 3 (1: -: -: -: -) rows, ending with a WS row.
All sizes
Dec 1 st at each end of next 1 (1: 1: 5: 5: 9) rows, then on every foll alt row until 37 (39: 39: 39: 41: 41) sts rem.
Work 1 row, ending with a WS row.
Shape back neck
Next row (RS): Work 2 tog, patt 3 sts and

turn, leaving rem sts on a holder.
Work each side of neck separately.
Dec 1 st at beg of next row.
Cast off rem 3 sts.
With RS facing, rejoin yarn to rem sts, cast off centre 27 (29: 29: 29: 31: 31) sts, patt to last 2 sts, work 2 tog. 4 sts.
Complete to match first side, reversing shapings.

FRONT

Work as given for back until 47 (51: 51: 51: 53: 53) sts rem in raglan armhole shaping.
Work 1 row, ending with a WS row.
Shape neck
Next row (RS): Work 2 tog, patt 16 (18: 18: 18: 18: 18) sts and turn, leaving rem sts on a holder.
Work each side of neck separately.
Cast off 5 sts at beg of next row. 12 (14: 14: 14: 14: 14) sts.
Dec 1 st at neck edge of next 5 rows, then on foll 1 (2: 2: 2: 2: 2) alt rows **and at same time** dec 1 st at raglan armhole edge of next and every foll alt row. 2 sts.
Work 1 row, ending with a WS row.
Next row (RS): K2tog and fasten off.
With RS facing, rejoin yarn to rem sts, cast off centre 11 (11: 11: 11: 13: 13) sts, patt to last 2 sts, work 2 tog.
Complete to match first side, reversing shapings.

SLEEVES

Cast on 47 (49: 49: 51: 53: 53) sts using 4mm (US 6) needles.
Row 1 (WS): Purl.
Row 2: P0 (1: 1: 2: 3: 3), *K2, P3, rep from * to last 2 (3: 3: 4: 5: 5) sts, K2, P0 (1: 1: 2: 3: 3).
These 2 rows form patt.
Work in patt for a further 3 rows, ending with a WS row.
Change to 4¹/₂mm (US 7) needles.
Cont in patt, shaping sides by inc 1 st at each end of next and every foll 4th row to 69 (71: 77: 77: 79: 85) sts, then on every foll 6th row

until there are 87 (89: 91: 93: 95: 97) sts, taking inc sts into patt.

Cont straight until sleeve measures 44 (44: 44: 45: 45: 45)cm/17¼ (17¼: 17¼: 17¾: 17¾: 17¾)in, ending with a WS row.

Shape raglan

Keeping patt correct, cast off 4 sts at beg of next 2 rows. 79 (81: 83: 85: 87: 89) sts.

Dec 1 st at each end of next and every foll alt row until 19 sts rem.

Work 1 row, ending with a WS row.

Left sleeve only

Dec 1 st at each end of next row, then cast off 4 sts at beg of foll row. 13 sts.

Dec 1 st at beg of next row, then cast off 6 sts at beg of foll row.

Right sleeve only

Cast off 5 sts at beg and dec 1 st at end of next row. 13 sts.

Work 1 row.

Cast off 6 sts at beg and dec 1 st at end of next row.

Work 1 row.

Both sleeves

Cast off rem 6 sts.

MAKING UP

PRESS as described on page 123.

Join both front and right back raglan seams using backstitch, or mattress stitch if preferred.

Collar

With RS facing and using 4mm (US 6) needles, pick up and knit 12 sts from left sleeve, 11 (15: 15: 15: 15: 15) sts down left side of neck, 13 (13: 13: 13: 16: 16) sts from front, 11 (15: 15: 15: 15: 15) sts up right side of neck, 12 sts from right sleeve, then 33 (35: 35: 35: 37: 37) sts from back. 92 (102: 102: 102: 107: 107) sts.

Row 1 (WS of body, RS of collar): K2, *P3, K2, rep from * to end.

Row 2: Purl.

These 2 rows form patt.

Cont in rib until collar measures 10cm/4in, ending with a WS row.

Change to 4½mm (US 7) needles.

Cont in patt until collar measures 20cm/7¾in.

Cast off in patt.

See page 124 for finishing instructions, reversing collar seam for turn-back.

TWEED PONCHO

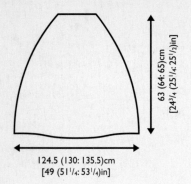

124.5 (130: 135.5)cm
[49 (51¹/₄: 53¹/₄)in]

63 (64: 65)cm
[24³/₄ (25¹/₄: 25¹/₂)in]

SIZES

| 1–2 | 3–4 | 5–6 |

TO FIT BUST

| 91–97 | 102–107 | 112–117 | cm |
| 36–38 | 40–42 | 44–46 | in |

YARN

Rowan Plaid – brown tweed (166)

| 10 | 11 | 12 | x 100gm |

NEEDLES

1 pair 8mm (no 0) (US 11) needles

TENSION

11 sts and 15 rows to 10cm/4in measured
over st st using 8mm (US 11) needles.

BACK AND FRONT (both alike)

Cast on 137 (143: 149) sts using 8mm (US
11) needles.
Work in garter st for 2 rows, ending with a
WS row.
Beg with a K row, work in st st for 14 rows,
ending with a WS row.
Place markers on 32nd (33rd: 34th) sts in from
both ends of last row.
Row 17 (RS): (K to within 2 sts of marked
st, K2tog tbl, K marked st, K2tog) twice, K
to end.
Row 18: Purl.
Rep rows 17 and 18, 17 (18: 19) times. 65 (67:
69) sts.
Next row (RS): As row 17.
Next row: Purl.
Next row: Knit.
Next row: Purl.
Rep last 4 rows 9 times more. 25 (27: 29) sts.
Rep rows 17 and 18 once.
Break yarn and leave rem 21 (23: 25) sts on
a holder.

MAKING UP

PRESS as described on page 123.
Join right shoulder and side seam using
backstitch, or mattress stitch if preferred.

Collar

With RS facing and using 8mm (US 11)
needles, K 21 (23: 25) sts of front, then K 21
(23: 25) sts of back. 42 (46: 50) sts.
Next row (WS): K2, *P2, K2, rep from *
to end.
Next row: P2, *K2, P2, rep from * to end.
Rep last 2 rows until collar measures
10cm/4in, ending with a WS row.
Next row (RS): P2, *K1, M1, K1, P2, rep
from * to end. 52 (57: 62) sts.
Next row: K2, *P3, K2, rep from * to end.
Next row: P2, *K3, P2, rep from * to end.
Rep last 2 rows until collar measures
22cm/8¾in.
Cast off in rib.
See page 124 for finishing instructions,
reversing collar seam for turn-back.
Cut 25cm/10in lengths of yarn and knot
groups of 3 of these lengths through every st
of cast-on and cast-off edges to form fringe.

ZIGZAG SCARF

YARNS

Rowan 4 ply Soft

A taupe (386)	3	x 50gm
B off-white (376)	3	x 50gm
C expresso (389)	2	x 50gm
D light dusty plum (378)	2	x 50gm

NEEDLES

1 pair 2¾mm (no 12) (US 2) needles
1 pair 3¼mm (no 10) (US 3) needles

TENSION

35 sts and 38 rows to 10cm/4in measured
over pattern using 3¼mm (US 3) needles.

FINISHED SIZE

Completed scarf measures 26cm/10in wide
and approx 204cm/80½in long, excluding fringe
at each end.

SCARF

First Section
Cast on 91 sts using 2¾mm (US 2) needles
and yarn A.
Row 1 (RS): K1, *yfwd, K3, K3tog, K3, yfwd,
K1, rep from * to end.
Row 2: Knit.
These 2 rows form patt.
Joining in and breaking off yarn as required,

cont in patt using colours as folls:
Rows 3 to 6: Using yarn A.
Change to 3¼mm (US 3) needles.
Rows 7 to 30: Using yarn A.
Rows 31 and 32: Using yarn B.
Rows 33 and 34: Using yarn A.
Rows 35 to 50: Rep rows 31 to 34
four times.
Rows 51 and 52: Using yarn B.
Rows 53 to 82: Using yarn C.
Rows 83 and 84: Using yarn B.
Rows 85 and 86: Using yarn A.
Rows 87 to 98: Rep rows 83 to 86
three times.
Rows 99 and 100: Using yarn B.
Rows 101 to 108: Using yarn C.
Rows 109 to 138: Using yarn D.
Rows 139 to 146: Using yarn C.
Rows 147 to 154: Using yarn D.
Rows 155 to 172: Using yarn C.
Rows 173 and 174: Using yarn A.
Rows 175 and 176: Using yarn B.
Rows 177 to 200: Rep rows 173 to 176
six times.
Rows 201 and 202: Using yarn A.
Rows 203 to 262: Using yarn B.
Rows 263 to 292: Using yarn A.
Rows 293 and 294: Using yarn B.
Rows 295 and 296: Using yarn A.
Rows 297 to 312: Rep rows 293 to 296
four times.
Rows 313 and 314: Using yarn B.
Rows 315 to 344: Using yarn C.
Rows 345 and 346: Using yarn B.
Rows 347 and 348: Using yarn A.
Rows 349 to 360: Rep rows 345 to 348
three times.
Rows 361 and 362: Using yarn B.
Rows 363 to 370: Using yarn C.
Rows 371 to 387: Using yarn D.**
Break yarn and leave sts on a holder.
Second section
Work as given for first section to **.
Join sections
Holding sections with RS facing, cast off both
sets of sts together by taking one st from

first section with corresponding st from
second section.

MAKING UP

PRESS as described on page 123.
Cut 32cm/12½in lengths of yarn A and knot
groups of 13 of these lengths through each
point of cast-on edges to form fringe.

BEADED JACKET & TEXTURED JACKET

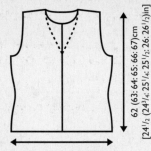

51.5 (54: 57: 59.5: 62.5: 65)cm
[20¹/₂ (21¹/₂: 22¹/₂: 23¹/₂: 24¹/₂: 25¹/₂)in]

62 (63: 64: 65: 66: 67)cm
[24¹/₂ (24³/₄: 25¹/₄: 25¹/₂: 26: 26¹/₂)in]

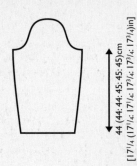

44 (44: 44: 45: 45: 45)cm
[17¹/₄ (17¹/₄: 17¹/₄: 17³/₄: 17³/₄: 17³/₄)in]

SIZES

| 1 | 2 | 3 | 4 | 5 | 6 |

TO FIT BUST

| 91 | 97 | 102 | 107 | 112 | 117 | cm |
| 36 | 38 | 40 | 42 | 44 | 46 | in |

YARNS

Jaeger Extra Fine Merino DK
BEADED VERSION – camel (938) – see left

| 13 | 13 | 14 | 14 | 15 | 15 x 50gm |

TEXTURED VERSION – ash (976) – see page 20

| 13 | 13 | 14 | 14 | 15 | 15 x 50gm |

NEEDLES

1 pair 3mm (no 11) (US 2/3) needles
1 pair 3¾mm (no 9) (US 5) needles

BUTTONS – 7 for beaded version, or 6 for textured version

BEADS – beaded version only: approx 1,060 (1,120: 1,180: 1,250: 1,310: 1,370) 2.5mm bronze-coloured glass beads (Rowan J3000-01009)

TENSION

22 sts and 30 rows to 10cm/4in measured over st st using 3¾mm (US 5) needles.

SPECIAL ABBREVIATION

bead 1 = place a bead by bringing yarn to RS of work and slipping bead up next to st just worked, slip next st purlwise from left needle to right needle and take yarn to WS of work, leaving bead sitting on RS of work in front of slipped st. Do not place beads on edge stitches of work as this will interfere with seaming.

Pattern note: Before starting to knit beaded jacket, thread beads onto yarn. To do this, thread a fine sewing needle (one that will easily pass through the beads) with sewing thread. Knot ends of thread and then pass end of yarn through this loop. Thread a bead onto

sewing thread and then gently slide it along and onto knitting yarn. Continue in this way until required number of beads are on yarn.

BACK

Cast on 113 (119: 125: 131: 137: 143) sts using 3mm (US 2/3) needles.
Row 1 (RS): K1 (0: 1: 0: 1: 0), *P1, K1, rep from * to last 0 (1: 0: 1: 0: 1) st, P0 (1: 0: 1: 0: 1).
Row 2: As row 1.
These 2 rows form moss st.
Cont in moss st for a further 8 rows, ending with a WS row.
Change to 3¾mm (US 5) needles.
Row 1 (RS): Knit.
Row 2 and every foll alt row: Purl.
Beaded version only
Row 3: K6 (9: 2: 5: 8: 1), *bead 1, K9, rep from * to last 7 (10: 3: 6: 9: 2) sts, bead 1, K6 (9: 2: 5: 8: 1).
Textured version only
Row 3: K6 (9: 2: 5: 8: 1), *P1, K9, rep from * to last 7 (10: 3: 6: 9: 2) sts, P1, K6 (9: 2: 5: 8: 1).
Both versions
Rows 5 and 7: Knit.
Beaded version only
Row 9: K1 (4: 7: 10: 3: 6), *bead 1, K9, rep from * to last 2 (5: 8: 11: 4: 7) sts, bead 1, K1 (4: 7: 10: 3: 6).
Textured version only
Row 9: K1 (4: 7: 10: 3: 6), *P1, K9, rep from * to last 2 (5: 8: 11: 4: 7) sts, P1, K1 (4: 7: 10: 3: 6).
Both versions
Row 11: Knit.
Row 12: Purl.
These 12 rows form patt.
Cont in patt, dec 1 st at each end of 15th (17th: 17th: 17th: 17th: 19th) and every foll 10th row to 107 (113: 119: 125: 131: 137) sts, then on every foll 8th row until there are 103 (109: 115: 121: 127: 133) sts.
Work 5 (7: 7: 7: 7: 9) rows, ending with a WS row.
Inc 1 st at each end of next and every foll 8th row until there are 113 (119: 125: 131: 137: 143) sts, taking inc sts into patt.

Cont straight until back measures 39 (40: 40: 41: 41: 42)cm/15½ (15¾: 15¾: 16: 16¼: 16¾)in, ending with a WS row.

Shape armholes

Keeping patt correct, cast off 5 (6: 6: 7: 7: 8) sts at beg of next 2 rows. 103 (107: 113: 117: 123: 127) sts.

Dec 1 st at each end of next 3 (3: 5: 5: 7: 7) rows, then on foll 3 (4: 4: 5: 5: 6) alt rows, then on every foll 4th row until 87 (89: 91: 93: 95: 97) sts rem.

Cont straight until armhole measures 23 (23: 24: 24: 25: 25)cm/9 (9: 9½: 9½: 9¾: 9¾)in, ending with a WS row.

Shape shoulders and back neck

Cast off 9 (9: 9: 9: 9: 10) sts at beg of next 2 rows. 69 (71: 73: 75: 77: 77) sts.

Next row (RS): Cast off 9 (9: 9: 9: 9: 10) sts, patt until there are 12 (12: 13: 14: 14: 13) sts on right needle and turn, leaving rem sts on a holder.

Work each side of neck separately.

Cast off 4 sts at beg of next row.

Cast off rem 8 (8: 9: 10: 10: 9) sts.

With RS facing, rejoin yarn to rem sts, cast off centre 27 (29: 29: 29: 31: 31) sts, patt to end.

Complete to match first side, reversing shapings.

LEFT FRONT

Cast on 65 (68: 71: 74: 77: 80) sts using 3mm (US 2/3) needles.

Row 1 (RS): K1 (0: 1: 0: 1: 0), *P1, K1, rep from * to end.

Row 2: K1, *P1, K1, rep from * to last 0 (1: 0: 1: 0: 1) st, P0 (1: 0: 1: 0: 1).

These 2 rows form moss st.

Cont in moss st for a further 7 rows, ending with a RS row.

Row 10 (WS): Moss st 8 sts and slip these sts onto a holder, moss st to end. 57 (60: 63: 66: 69: 72) sts.

Change to 3¾mm (US 5) needles.

Row 1 (RS): Knit.

Row 2 and every foll alt row: Purl.

Beaded version only

Row 3: K6 (9: 2: 5: 8: 1), *bead 1, K9, rep from * to last st, K1.

Textured version only

Row 3: K6 (9: 2: 5: 8: 1), *P1, K9, rep from * to last st, K1.

Both versions

Rows 5 and 7: Knit.

Beaded version only

Row 9: K1 (4: 7: 10: 3: 6), *bead 1, K9, rep from * to last 6 sts, bead 1, K5.

Textured version only

Row 9: K1 (4: 7: 10: 3: 6), *P1, K9, rep from * to last 6 sts, P1, K5.

Both versions

Row 11: Knit.

Row 12: Purl.

These 12 rows form patt.

Cont in patt, dec 1 st at beg of 15th (17th: 17th: 17th: 17th: 19th) and every foll 10th row to 54 (57: 60: 63: 66: 69) sts, then on every foll 8th row until there are 52 (55: 58: 61: 64: 67) sts.

Work 5 (7: 7: 7: 7: 9) rows, ending with a WS row.

Inc 1 st at beg of next and every foll 8th row until there are 57 (60: 63: 66: 69: 72) sts, taking inc sts into patt.

Cont straight until left front matches back to beg of armhole shaping, ending with a WS row.

Shape armhole

Keeping patt correct, cast off 5 (6: 6: 7: 7: 8) sts at beg of next row. 52 (54: 57: 59: 62: 64) sts.

Work 1 row.

Beaded version only

Dec 1 st at armhole edge of next 3 (3: 5: 5: 7: 7) rows, then on foll 3 (4: 4: 5: 5: 6) alt rows, then on every foll 4th row until 44 (45: 46: 47: 48: 49) sts rem.

Cont straight until 15 (17: 17: 17: 17: 17) rows less have been worked than on back to start of shoulder shaping, ending with a RS row.

Shape neck

Keeping patt correct, cast off 9 (9: 9: 9: 10: 10) sts at beg of next row. 35 (36: 37: 38: 38: 39) sts.

Dec 1 st at neck edge of next 6 rows, then on foll 2 (3: 3: 3: 3: 3) alt rows, then on foll 4th row, ending with a WS row.

Textured version only

Dec 1 st at armhole edge of next 3 (3: 4: 4: 4: 4) rows. 49 (51: 53: 55: 58: 60) sts.

Work 1 (1: 0: 0: 0: 0) row, ending with a WS row.

Shape front slope

Dec 1 st at armhole edge of next 1 (1: 1: 1: 3: 3) rows, then on foll 2 (3: 4: 5: 5: 6) alt rows, then on 2 foll 4th rows **and at same time** dec 1 st at front slope edge on next and foll 6 (7: 8: 8: 8: 8) alt rows, then on foll 0 (0: 0: 0: 4th: 4th) row. 37 (37: 37: 38: 38: 39) sts.

Dec 1 st at front slope edge only on 2nd (2nd: 4th: 2nd: 4th: 2nd) and foll 0 (1: 0: 0: 0: 0) alt row, then on every foll 4th row until 26 (26: 27: 28: 28: 29) sts rem.

Cont straight until left front matches back to start of shoulder shaping, ending with a WS row.

Both versions

Shape shoulder

Cast off 9 (9: 9: 9: 9: 10) sts at beg of next and foll alt row. Work 1 row.

Cast off rem 8 (8: 9: 10: 10: 9) sts.

RIGHT FRONT

Cast on 65 (68: 71: 74: 77: 80) sts using 3mm (US 2/3) needles.

Row 1 (RS): K1, *P1, K1, rep from * to last 0 (1: 0: 1: 0: 1) st, P0 (1: 0: 1: 0: 1).

Row 2: K1 (0: 1: 0: 1: 0), *P1, K1, rep from * to end.

These 2 rows form moss st.

Cont in moss st for a further 2 rows, ending with a WS row.

Row 5 (RS): K1, P1, K1, P2tog, yrn (to make a buttonhole), moss st to end.

Cont in moss st for a further 4 rows, ending with a RS row.

Row 10 (WS): Moss st to last 8 sts and turn, leaving rem 8 sts on a holder. 57 (60: 63: 66: 69: 72) sts.

Change to 3¾mm (US 5) needles.

Row 1 (RS): Knit.

Row 2 and every foll alt row: Purl.
Beaded version only
Row 3: K10, *bead 1, K9, rep from * to last 7 (10: 3: 6: 9: 2) sts, bead 1, K6 (9: 2: 5: 8: 1).
Textured version only
Row 3: K10, *P1, K9, rep from * to last 7 (10: 3: 6: 9: 2) sts, P1, K6 (9: 2: 5: 8: 1).
Both versions
Rows 5 and 7: Knit.
Beaded version only
Row 9: K5, *bead 1, K9, rep from * to last 2 (5: 8: 11: 4: 7) sts, bead 1, K1 (4: 7: 10: 3: 6).
Textured version only
Row 9: K5, *P1, K9, rep from * to last 2 (5: 8: 11: 4: 7) sts, P1, K1 (4: 7: 10: 3: 6).
Both versions
Row 11: Knit.
Row 12: Purl.
These 12 rows form patt.
Cont in patt, dec 1 st at end of 15th (17th: 17th: 17th: 17th: 19th) and every foll 10th row to 54 (57: 60: 63: 66: 69) sts, then on every foll 8th row until there are 52 (55: 58: 61: 64: 67) sts.
Complete to match left front, reversing shapings.

SLEEVES (both alike)

Cast on 57 (59: 59: 61: 63: 63) sts using 3mm (US 2/3) needles.
Row 1 (RS): K1, *P1, K1, rep from * to end.
Row 2: As row 1.
These 2 rows form moss st.
Cont in moss st for a further 8 rows, ending with a WS row.
Change to 3¾mm (US 5) needles.
Row 1 (RS): Inc in first st, K to last st, inc in last st. 59 (61: 61: 63: 65: 65) sts.
Row 2 and every foll alt row: Purl.
Beaded version only
Row 3: K9 (10: 10: 1: 2: 2), *bead 1, K9, rep from * to last 10 (11: 11: 2: 3: 3) sts, bead 1, K9 (10: 10: 1: 2: 2).
Textured version only
Row 3: K9 (10: 10: 1: 2: 2), *P1, K9, rep from * to last 10 (11: 11: 2: 3: 3) sts, P1, K9 (10: 10: 1: 2: 2).

Both versions
Row 5: Knit.
Row 7: (Inc in first st) 0 (0: 1: 1: 1: 1) times, K to last 0 (0: 1: 1: 1: 1) st, (inc in last st) 0 (0: 1: 1: 1: 1) times. 59 (61: 63: 65: 67: 67) sts.
Beaded version only
Row 9: (Inc in first st) 1 (1: 0: 0: 0: 0) times, K3 (4: 6: 7: 8: 8), *bead 1, K9, rep from * to last 5 (6: 7: 8: 9: 9) sts, bead 1, K3 (4: 6: 7: 8: 8), (inc in last st) 1 (1: 0: 0: 0: 0) times. 61 (63: 63: 65: 67: 67) sts.
Textured version only
Row 9: (Inc in first st) 1 (1: 0: 0: 0: 0) times, K3 (4: 6: 7: 8: 8), *P1, K9, rep from * to last 5 (6: 7: 8: 9: 9) sts, P1, K3 (4: 6: 7: 8: 8), (inc in last st) 1 (1: 0: 0: 0: 0) times. 61 (63: 63: 65: 67: 67) sts.
Both versions
Row 11: Knit.
Row 12: Purl.
These 12 rows form patt and start sleeve shaping.
Cont in patt, inc 1 st at each end of 5th (5th: next: 3rd: 3rd: next) and every foll 8th (8th: 8th: 8th: 8th: 6th) row to 81 (83: 89: 91: 93: 75) sts, then on every foll 10th (10th: -: -: -: 8th) row until there are 85 (87: -: -: -: 95) sts, taking inc sts into patt.
Cont straight until sleeve measures 44 (44: 44: 45: 45: 45)cm/17¼ (17¼: 17¼: 17¾: 17¾: 17¾)in, ending with a WS row.

Shape top

Keeping patt correct, cast off 5 (6: 6: 7: 7: 8) sts at beg of next 2 rows. 75 (75: 77: 77: 79: 79) sts.
Dec 1 st at each end of next 5 rows, then on foll 4 alt rows, then on every foll 4th row until 49 (49: 51: 51: 53: 53) sts rem.
Work 1 row, ending with a WS row.
Dec 1 st at each end of next and every foll alt row to 39 sts, then on foll 3 rows, ending with a WS row.
Cast off 5 sts at beg of next 2 rows.
Cast off rem 23 sts.

MAKING UP

PRESS as described on page 123.
Join both shoulder seams using backstitch.

Beaded version only
Left front band

Slip 8 sts from left front holder onto 3mm (US 2/3) needles and rejoin yarn with RS facing.
Cont in moss st as set until band, when slightly stretched, fits up left front opening edge to neck shaping, ending with a WS row.
Break yarn and leave sts on a holder.
Slip stitch band in place.
Mark positions for 7 buttons on this band section – first to come level with buttonhole already worked in right front, last to come just above neck shaping, and rem 5 buttons evenly spaced between.

Right front band

Slip 8 sts from right front holder onto 3mm (US 2/3) needles and rejoin yarn with WS facing.
Cont in moss st as set until band, when slightly stretched, fits up right front opening edge to neck shaping, ending with a WS row and with the addition of a further 5 buttonholes worked as folls:
Buttonhole row (RS): K1, P1, K1, P2tog, yrn (to make a buttonhole), P1, K1, P1.
When band is complete, do NOT break off yarn.
Slip stitch band in place.

Collar

With RS facing and using 3mm (US 2/3) needles, moss st 8 sts from right front band, pick up and knit 21 (23: 23: 23: 24: 24) sts up right side of neck, 35 (37: 37: 37: 39: 39) sts from back, and 21 (23: 23: 23: 24: 24) sts down left side of neck, then moss st 8 sts from left front band. 93 (99: 99: 99: 103: 103) sts.
Work in moss st as set by bands for 3 rows, ending with a WS row.
Next row (RS of body): K1, P1, K1, P2tog, yrn (to make 7th buttonhole), moss st to end.
Work in moss st for a further 4 rows.
Cast off 4 sts at beg of next 2 rows. 85 (91: 91: 91: 95: 95) sts.
Cont in moss st until collar measures 12cm/4¾in from pick-up row.
Cast off in moss st.

Textured version only

Place markers along front slope edges 9cm/3½in below shoulder seams.

Left front band and collar

Slip 8 sts from left front holder onto 3mm (US 2/3) needles and rejoin yarn with RS facing.

Cont in moss st as set until band, when slightly stretched, fits up left front opening edge to start of front slope shaping, ending with a WS row.

Shape for collar

Next row (RS of body, WS of collar section): Moss st 1 st, inc twice in next st (by working into front, back and front again of st), moss st to end. 10 sts.

Work 5 rows.

Rep last 6 rows 6 times more. 22 sts.

Cont straight until collar section, unstretched, fits up front slope to marker, ending at outer (unshaped) edge.

Next row (RS of collar): Cast off 9 sts, turn and cast on 9 sts, turn and moss st to end. 22 sts.

Cont straight until collar section, unstretched, fits up rem section of front slope and across to centre back neck, ending with a WS row.

Cast off in moss st.

Slip stitch band and collar in place.

Mark positions for 6 buttons on this band section – first to come level with buttonhole already worked in right front, last to come 1cm/½in below start of front slope shaping, and rem 4 buttons evenly spaced between.

Right front band and collar

Slip 8 sts from right front holder onto 3mm (US 2/3) needles and rejoin yarn with WS facing.

Cont in moss st as set until right front band, when slightly stretched, fits up right front opening edge to start of front slope shaping, ending with a WS row and with the addition of a further 5 buttonholes worked as folls:

Buttonhole row (RS): K1, P1, K1, P2tog, yrn (to make a buttonhole), P1, K1, P1.

Shape for collar

Next row (RS of body, WS of collar section): Moss st to last 2 sts, inc twice in next st, moss st 1 st. 10 sts.

Work 5 rows.

Rep last 6 rows 6 times more. 22 sts.

Cont straight until collar section, unstretched, fits up front slope to marker, ending at outer (unshaped) edge.

Next row (WS of collar): Cast off 9 sts, turn and cast on 9 sts, turn and moss st to end. 22 sts.

Cont straight until collar section, unstretched, fits up rem section of front slope and across to centre back neck, ending with a WS row.

Cast off in moss st.

Slip stitch band and collar in place, joining cast-off ends of collar sections.

Both versions

See page 124 for finishing instructions, setting in sleeves using the set-in method.

DIAMOND-PATTERN SWEATER

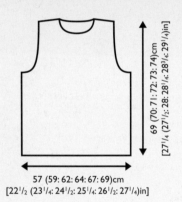

57 (59: 62: 64: 67: 69)cm
[22½ (23¼: 24½: 25¼: 26½: 27¼)in]

69 (70: 71: 71: 72: 73: 74)cm
[27¼ (27½: 28: 28¼: 28¾: 29¼)in]

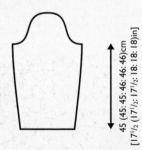

45 (45: 45: 46: 46: 46)cm
[17½ (17½: 17½: 18: 18: 18)in]

SIZES

1	2	3	4	5	6

TO FIT BUST

| 91 | 97 | 102 | 107 | 112 | 117 | cm |
| 36 | 38 | 40 | 42 | 44 | 46 | in |

YARN

Rowan 4 ply Soft – dark grey (372)

| 11 | 11 | 12 | 12 | 13 | 13 x 50gm |

NEEDLES

1 pair 2¾mm (no 12) (US 2) needles
1 pair 3¼mm (no 10) (US 3) needles

TENSION

28 sts and 36 rows to 10cm/4in measured over st st using 3¼mm (US 3) needles.

BACK

Cast on 159 (165: 173: 179: 187: 193) sts using 2¾mm (US 2) needles.

Row 1 (RS): (K1 tbl) 3 (3: 4: 4: 2: 2) times, *(P1 tbl) 3 times, (K1 tbl) 3 times, rep from * to last 0 (0: 1: 1: 5: 5) sts, (P1 tbl) 0 (0: 0: 0: 3: 3) times, (K1 tbl) 0 (0: 1: 1: 2: 2) times.

Row 2: (P1 tbl) 3 (3: 4: 4: 2: 2) times, *(K1 tbl) 3 times, (P1 tbl) 3 times, rep from * to last 0 (0: 1: 1: 5: 5) sts, (K1 tbl) 0 (0: 0: 0: 3: 3) times, (P1 tbl) 0 (0: 1: 1: 2: 2) times.

These 2 rows form twisted rib.

Cont in twisted rib for 13cm/5in, ending with a WS row.

Change to 3¼mm (US 3) needles.

Beg and ending rows as indicated and rep the 36 row patt rep throughout, cont in patt from chart until back measures 46 (47: 47: 48: 48: 49)cm/18¼ (18½: 18½: 18¾: 19: 19½)in, ending with a WS row.

Shape armholes

Keeping patt correct, cast off 8 (9: 9: 10: 10: 11) sts at beg of next 2 rows. 143 (147: 155: 159: 167: 171) sts.

Dec 1 st at each end of next 9 (9: 11: 11: 13: 13) rows, then on foll 7 (8: 8: 9: 9: 10) alt rows, then on foll 4th row. 109 (111: 115: 117: 121: 123) sts.

Cont straight until armhole measures 23 (23: 24: 24: 25: 25)cm/9 (9: 9½: 9½: 9¾: 9¾)in, ending with a WS row.

Shape shoulders and back neck

Cast off 10 (10: 11: 11: 11: 12) sts at beg of next 2 rows. 89 (91: 93: 95: 99: 99) sts.

Next row (RS): Cast off 10 (10: 11: 11: 11: 12) sts, patt until there are 14 (14: 14: 15: 16: 15) sts on right needle and turn, leaving rem sts on a holder.

Work each side of neck separately.

Cast off 4 sts at beg of next row.

Cast off rem 10 (10: 10: 11: 12: 11) sts.

With RS facing, rejoin yarn to rem sts, cast off centre 41 (43: 43: 43: 45: 45) sts, patt to end.

Complete to match first side, reversing shapings.

FRONT

Work as given for back until 20 (22: 22: 22: 22: 22) rows less have been worked than on back to start of shoulder shaping, ending with a WS row.

Shape neck

Next row (RS): Patt 42 (43: 45: 46: 47: 48) sts and turn, leaving rem sts on a holder.

Work each side of neck separately.

Dec 1 st at neck edge of next 7 rows, then on foll 4 (5: 5: 5: 5: 5) alt rows, then on foll 4th row, ending with a WS row. 30 (30: 32: 33: 34: 35) sts.

Shape shoulder

Cast off 10 (10: 11: 11: 11: 12) sts at beg of next and foll alt row.

Work 1 row.

Cast off rem 10 (10: 10: 11: 12: 11) sts.

With RS facing, rejoin yarn to rem sts, cast off centre 25 (25: 25: 25: 27: 27) sts, patt to end.

Complete to match first side, reversing shapings.

SLEEVES (both alike)

Cast on 65 (67: 67: 69: 71: 71) sts using 2¾mm (US 2) needles.

Row 1 (RS): (P1 tbl) 1 (2: 2: 3: 1: 1) times, *(K1 tbl) 3 times, (P1 tbl) 3 times, rep from * to last 4 (5: 5: 6: 4: 4) sts, (K1 tbl) 3 times, (P1 tbl) 1 (2: 2: 3: 1: 1) times.

Row 2: (K1 tbl) 1 (2: 2: 3: 1: 1) times, *(P1 tbl) 3 times, (K1 tbl) 3 times, rep from * to last 4 (5: 5: 6: 4: 4) sts, (P1 tbl) 3 times, (K1 tbl) 1 (2: 2: 3: 1: 1) times.

These 2 rows form twisted rib.

Cont in twisted rib for a further 28 rows, ending with a WS row.

Change to 3¼mm (US 3) needles.

Beg and ending rows as indicated and rep the 36 row patt rep throughout, cont in patt from chart, shaping sides by inc 1 st at each end of next and every foll 4th row to 79 (81: 93: 91: 99: 105) sts, then on every foll 6th row until there are 109 (111: 115: 117: 121: 123) sts, taking inc sts into patt.

Cont straight until sleeve measures 45 (45: 45: 46: 46: 46)cm/17½ (17½: 17½: 18: 18: 18)in, ending with a WS row.

Shape top

Keeping patt correct, cast off 8 (9: 9: 10: 10: 11) sts at beg of next 2 rows. 93 (93: 97: 97: 101: 101) sts.

Dec 1 st at each end of next 11 rows, then on foll 7 alt rows, then on every foll 4th row until 51 (51: 55: 55: 59: 59) sts rem.

Work 1 row, ending with a WS row.

Dec 1 st at each end of next and every foll alt row to 43 sts, then on foll 7 rows, ending with a WS row.

Cast off rem 29 sts.

MAKING UP

PRESS as described on page 123.

Join right shoulder seam using backstitch, or mattress stitch if preferred.

Collar

With RS facing and using 2¾mm (US 2) needles, pick up and knit 24 (26: 26: 26: 27: 27) sts down left side of neck, 26 (26: 26: 26: 28: 28) sts from front, 24 (26: 26: 26: 27: 27) sts up right side of neck, then 49 (51: 51: 51: 53: 53) sts from back. 123 (129: 129: 129: 135: 135) sts.

Row 1 (WS): (P1 tbl) 3 times, *(K1 tbl) 3 times, (P1 tbl) 3 times, rep from * to end.

Row 2: (K1 tbl) 3 times, *(P1 tbl) 3 times, (K1 tbl) 3 times, rep from * to end.

These 2 rows form rib.

Cont in rib until collar measures 10cm/4in, ending with a WS row.

Next row (RS): (K1 tbl) 3 times, *(P1 tbl) twice, M1P, P1 tbl, (K1 tbl) 3 times, rep from * to end. 143 (150: 150: 150: 157: 157) sts.

Next row: (P1 tbl) 3 times, *(K1 tbl) 4 times, (P1 tbl) 3 times, rep from * to end.

Next row: (K1 tbl) 3 times, *(P1 tbl) 4 times, (K1 tbl) 3 times, rep from * to end.

Change to 3¼mm (US 3) needles.

Rep last 2 rows until collar measures 21cm/8¼in.

Cast off in rib.

See page 124 for finishing instructions, setting in sleeves using the set-in method.

Key ▫ K on RS, P on WS ▪ P on RS, K on WS

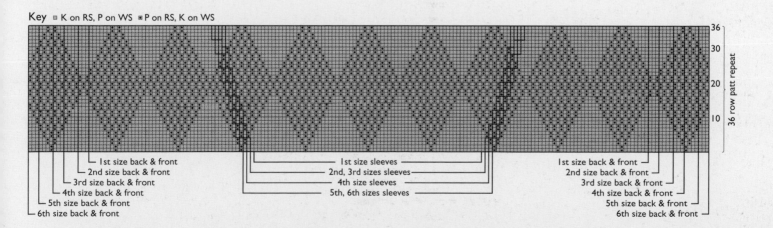

RICH COLOURS

This deeper colour palette in
autumnal shades of burgundy, plum
and mauve is sophisticated and
smart, yet feminine and appealing.
Flattering fluted collars abound, along
with jazzy accessories, including a
great looped bag and funky hat!
Yarns in this section include soft
mohairs and cottons.

Left *The neat, loose-fitting, hip-length Casual Sweater, knitted in stocking stitch in a super-soft cotton, has garter-stitch cuffs and collar. (Instructions on page 112.)*

Right *The very simple, dressy Mesh Scarf is crocheted in a lightweight cotton yarn and has a fluted trim in a contrasting colour. It is shown here with the Round-neck Top. (Instructions for scarf on page 122 and for top on page 78.)*

Right *The Loop-collar Sweater, knitted in a cotton yarn, has a face-framing neckline with its deep rolled, loop-fringed collar and matching cuffs. It can be worn casually witih jeans or dressed up for the evening. (Instructions on page 116)*

Far right *The Cable-rib Sweater, also knitted in cotton yarn, is a great long-length textured sweater for easy living. (Instructions on page 118.)*

Left and above In a soft mohair-mix yarn, the Loop-stitch Scarf, Bag and Hat make a great matching set and are fun to wear and to knit. Once you have mastered the looped knitting, the rest is plain sailing. (Instructions on page 114.)

Left *The Lace-frill Jacket is a really versatile short coat or long jacket. Ideal for wearing over smart trousers or a long skirt, it is knitted in an Aran-weight merino wool. The prettily ruffled edge, in a matching mohair/silk yarn, runs right around the front and hem. (Instructions on page 120.)*

CASUAL SWEATER

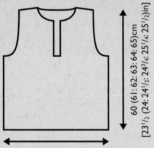

52 (55: 57.5: 60.5: 63.5: 66)cm
[20¹/₂ (21¹/₂: 22¹/₂: 24: 25: 26)in]

60 (61: 62: 63: 64: 65)cm
[23¹/₂ (24: 24¹/₂: 24³/₄: 25¹/₄: 25¹/₂)in]

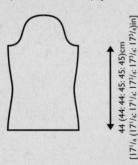

44 (44: 44: 45: 45: 45)cm
[17¹/₄ (17¹/₄: 17¹/₄: 17³/₄: 17³/₄: 17³/₄)in]

SIZES

1	2	3	4	5	6

TO FIT BUST

| 91 | 97 | 102 | 107 | 112 | 117 | cm |
| 36 | 38 | 40 | 42 | 44 | 46 | in |

YARN
Rowan Calmer – dark purple (478)

8	8	9	9	10	10 x 50gm

NEEDLES
1 pair 5mm (no 6) (US 8) needles
1 pair 4mm (no 8) (US 6) needles

TENSION
21 sts and 30 rows to 10cm/4in measured over st st using 5mm (US 8) needles.

BACK
Cast on 109 (115: 121: 127: 133: 139) sts using 4mm (US 8) needles.
Work in garter st for 4 rows, ending with a WS row.
Change to 5mm (US 8) needles.
Row 5 (RS): Knit.
Row 6: K3, P to last 3 sts, K3.
Rep last 2 rows 11 times, ending with a WS row.
Beg with a K row, cont in st st until back measures 37 (38: 38: 39: 39: 40)cm/14½ (15: 15: 15¼: 15½: 15¾)in, ending with a WS row.
Shape armholes
Cast off 6 (7: 7: 8: 8: 9) sts at beg of next 2 rows. 97 (101: 107: 111: 117: 121) sts.
Dec 1 st at each end of next 5 (5: 7: 7: 9: 9) rows, then on foll 3 (4: 4: 5: 5: 6) alt rows, then on every foll 4th row until 77 (79: 81: 83: 85: 87) sts rem.**
Cont straight until armhole measures 23 (23: 24: 24: 25: 25)cm/9 (9: 9½: 9½: 9¾: 9¾)in, ending with a WS row.
Shape shoulders and back neck
Cast off 6 (6: 7: 7: 7: 7) sts at beg of next 2 rows. 65 (67: 67: 69: 71: 73) sts.
Next row (RS): Cast off 6 (6: 7: 7: 7: 7) sts, K until there are 11 (11: 10: 11: 11: 12) sts on right needle and turn, leaving rem sts on a holder.
Work each side of neck separately.
Cast off 4 sts at beg of next row.
Cast off rem 7 (7: 6: 7: 7: 8) sts.
With RS facing, rejoin yarn to rem sts, cast off centre 31 (33: 33: 33: 35: 35) sts, K to end.
Complete to match first side, reversing shapings.

FRONT
Work as given for back to **.
***Work 3 (1: 3: 1: 3: 1) rows, ending with a WS row.
Divide for front opening
Next row (RS): K36 (37: 38: 39: 40: 41) and turn, leaving rem sts on a holder.
Work each side of neck separately.
Cont straight until 17 (19: 19: 19: 19: 19) rows less have been worked than on back to start of shoulder shaping, ending with a RS row.
Shape neck
Cast off 8 (8: 8: 8: 9: 9) sts at beg of next row. 28 (29: 30: 31: 31: 32) sts.
Dec 1 st at neck edge of next 6 rows, then on foll 1 (2: 2: 2: 2: 2) alt rows, then on every foll 4th row until 19 (19: 20: 21: 21: 22) sts rem, ending with a WS row.
Shape shoulder
Cast off 6 (6: 7: 7: 7: 7) sts at beg of next and foll alt row.
Work 1 row.
Cast off rem 7 (7: 6: 7: 7: 8) sts.
With RS facing, slip centre 5 sts onto a holder, rejoin yarn to rem sts, K to end.
Complete to match first side, reversing shapings.

SLEEVES (both alike)
Cast on 79 (81: 81: 83: 85: 85) sts using 4mm (US 6) needles.
Work in garter st for 4 rows, ending with a WS row.
Change to 5mm (US 8) needles.
Row 5 (RS): Knit.

Row 6: K3, P to last 3 sts, K3.

Rows 7 to 10: As rows 5 and 6 twice.

Row 11: K3, K2tog, K to last 5 sts, sl 1, K1, psso, K3.

Row 12: As row 6.

Rows 13 to 16: As rows 5 and 6 twice.

Rep last 6 rows twice more. 73 (75: 75: 77: 79: 79) sts.

Beg with a K row, cont in st st, dec 1 st at each end of 7th and every foll 6th row until 61 (63: 63: 65: 67: 67) sts rem.

Work 5 rows, ending with a WS row.

Inc 1 st at each end of next and every foll 6th (6th: 6th: 6th: 6th: 4th) row to 71 (73: 81: 81: 83: 73) sts, then on every foll 8th (8th: -: 8th: 8th: 6th) row until there are 77 (79: -: 83: 85: 87) sts.

Cont straight until sleeve measures 44 (44: 44: 45: 45: 45)cm/17¼ (17¼: 17¼: 17¾: 17¾: 17¾)in, ending with a WS row.

Shape top

Cast off 6 (7: 7: 8: 8: 9) sts at beg of next 2 rows. 65 (65: 67: 67: 69: 69) sts.

Dec 1 st at each end of next 7 rows, then on every foll alt row to 45 sts, then on every foll 4th row until 33 sts rem.

Work 1 row, ending with a WS row.

Dec 1 st at each end of next 6 rows, ending with a WS row.

Cast off rem 21 sts.

MAKING UP

PRESS as described on page 123.

Join both shoulder seams using backstitch, or mattress stitch if preferred.

Left front border

Cast on 5 sts using 4mm (US 6) needles.

Work in garter st until border, when slightly stretched, fits up left side of front opening, from base of opening to neck shaping, ending with a WS row.

Break yarn and leave sts on a holder.

Right front border

Slip 5 sts left on holder at base of front opening onto 4mm (US 8) needles and rejoin yarn with RS facing.

Work in garter st until border, when slightly stretched, fits up right side of front opening to neck shaping, ending with a WS row.

Do NOT break yarn.

Slip stitch borders in place, sewing cast-on edge of left front border to WS behind pick-up row of right front border.

Collar

With RS facing and using 4mm (US 6) needles, K 5 sts of right front border, pick up and knit 24 (26: 26: 26: 27: 27) sts up right side of neck, 39 (41: 41: 41: 43: 43) sts from back, and 24 (26: 26: 26: 27: 27) sts down left side of neck, then K 5 sts of left front border. 97 (103: 103: 103: 107: 107) sts.

Cont in garter st until collar measures 12cm/4¾in, ending with RS of body facing for next row.

Cast off knitwise.

See page 124 for finishing instructions, setting in sleeves using the set-in method and leaving side and sleeve seams open for first 28 rows.

LOOP-STITCH SCARF & BAG

YARN
Rowan Kid Classic – lavender ice (841)
SCARF
7 x 50gm
BAG
5 x 50gm

NEEDLES
1 pair 4½mm (no 7) (US 7) needles
Bag only: 1 pair 4mm (no 8) (US 6) needles

EXTRAS – bag only: piece of lining fabric
40cm x 70cm/16in x28in; same size piece of
polyester wadding; sewing thread.

TENSION
16 sts and 25 rows to 10cm/4in measured
over pattern using 4½mm (US 7) needles.

FINISHED SIZE
Completed scarf measures 26cm/10in wide
and 180cm/71in long.
Completed bag measures 26cm/10in wide and
26cm/10in deep.

SPECIAL ABBREVIATIONS
make loop = K1 leaving st on left needle,
bring yarn to front of work between needles
and wrap it twice round thumb of left hand,

take yarn back to WS of work between
needles and K same st again, letting st slip off
left needle, bring yarn to front of work
between needles and take it back to WS over
right needle point, lift last 2 sts on right needle
over this loop and off right needle.

LOOP STITCH SCARF

TO MAKE
Cast on 41 sts using 4½mm (US 7) needles.
Row 1 (WS): Knit.
Row 2: K1, *make loop, K1, rep from * to end.
Row 3: Knit.
Row 4: K2, *make loop, K1, rep from * to last
st, K1.
These 4 rows form patt.
Cont in patt until scarf measures 180cm/71in,
ending with a RS row.
Cast off knitwise (on WS).

MAKING UP
PRESS as described on page 123.

LOOP STITCH BAG

SIDES (make 2)
Cast on 41 sts using 4½mm (US 7) needles.
**Row 1 (WS): Knit.
Row 2: K1, *make loop, K1, rep from * to end.
Row 3: Knit.
Row 4: K2, *make loop, K1, rep from * to last
st, K1.
These 4 rows form patt.
Cont in patt until side measures 25cm/9¾in,
ending with a RS row.
Change to 4mm (US 6) needles.
Work in garter st for 4 rows.
Cast off knitwise (on WS).

GUSSETS (make 2)
Cast on 17 sts using 4½mm (US 7) needles.
Complete the gusset as given for sides
from **.

BASE
Cast on 17 sts using 4½mm (US 7) needles.
Cont in patt as given for sides until base
measures 26cm/10¼in, ending with a RS row.
Cast off knitwise (on WS).

HANDLES (make 2)
Cast on 21 sts using 4mm (US 6) needles.
Row 1 (RS): K6, sLIP, K7, sLIP, K6.
Row 2: Purl.
Rep these 2 rows until handle measures
36cm/14¼in, ending with a WS row.
Cast off.

MAKING UP
PRESS as described on page 123.
From lining fabric, cut out sides, gussets and
base, adding seam allowance along all edges.
Cut out same pieces from wadding and tack
wadding to WS of lining fabric pieces. Join sides
to gussets, matching cast-on and cast-off edges.
Sew base to cast-on edges. Fold handles along
slip stitch lines and join seam. Attach ends of
handles to inside of upper (cast-off) edge of
sides, positioning handles 7cm/2¾in apart.
Make up lining sections in same way as knitted
sections. Fold seam allowance to WS around
upper edge. Slip lining inside bag and slip stitch
in place around upper opening edge.

LOOP-STITCH HAT

YARN

Rowan Kid Classic – lavender ice (841)
2 x 50gm

NEEDLES

1 pair 4½mm (no 7) (US 7) needles

TENSION

16 sts and 25 rows to 10cm/4in measured
over pattern using 4½mm (US 7) needles.

FINISHED SIZE

Completed hat measures 51cm/20in around
head.

SPECIAL ABBREVIATIONS

make loop = K1 leaving st on left needle,
bring yarn to front of work between needles
and wrap it twice round thumb of left hand,
take yarn back to WS of work between
needles and K same st again, letting st slip off
left needle, bring yarn to front of work
between needles and take it back to WS over
right needle point, lift last 2 sts on right needle
over this loop and off right needle.

HAT

Cast on 81 sts using 4½mm (US 7) needles.
Row 1 (WS): Knit.

Row 2: K1, *make loop, K1, rep from *
to end.
Row 3: Knit.
Row 4: K2, *make loop, K1, rep from * to last
st, K1.
These 4 rows form patt.
Cont in patt until hat measures 13cm/5in,
ending with a RS row.
Shape crown
Row 1 (WS): *K8, K2tog, rep from * to last
st, K1. 73 sts.
Work 1 row.
Row 3: *K7, K2tog, rep from * to last st, K1.
65 sts.
Work 1 row.
Row 5: *K6, K2tog, rep from * to last st, K1.
57 sts.
Work 1 row.
Row 7: *K5, K2tog, rep from * to last st, K1.
49 sts.
Work 1 row.
Row 9: *K4, K2tog, rep from * to last st, K1.
41 sts.
Work 1 row.
Row 11: *K3, K2tog, rep from * to last st, K1.
33 sts.
Work 1 row.
Row 13: *K2, K2tog, rep from * to last st, K1.
25 sts.
Work 1 row.
Row 15: K1, (K2tog) 12 times.
Break yarn and thread through rem 13 sts. Pull
up tight and fasten off securely.

MAKING UP

PRESS as described on page 123.
Join crown and back seam.

LOOP-COLLAR SWEATER

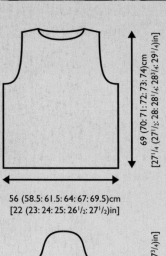

56 (58.5: 61.5: 64: 67: 69.5)cm
[22 (23: 24: 25: 26½: 27½)in]

69 (70: 71: 72: 73: 74)cm
[27¼ (27½: 28: 28¼: 28¾: 29¼)in]

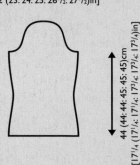

44 (44: 44: 45: 45: 45)cm
[17¼ (17¼: 17¼: 17¾: 17¾: 17¾)in]

SIZES

| 1 | 2 | 3 | 4 | 5 | 6 |

TO FIT BUST

| 91 | 97 | 102 | 107 | 112 | 117 | cm |
| 36 | 38 | 40 | 42 | 44 | 46 | in |

YARN

Rowan All Seasons Cotton – dark plum (181)

| 16 | 16 | 17 | 18 | 18 | 19 x 50gm |

NEEDLES AND CROCHET HOOK

1 pair 4mm (no 8) (US 6) needles
1 pair 4½mm (no 7) (US 7) needles
3.50mm (no 9) (US E-4) crochet hook

TENSION

18 sts and 25 rows to 10cm/4in measured over st st using 4½mm (US 7) needles.

CROCHET ABBREVIATIONS

ch = chain; **dc** = double crochet; **ss** = slip stitch.

BACK

Cast on 101 (105: 111: 115: 121: 125) sts using 4mm (US 6) needles.
Work in garter st for 4 rows, ending with a WS row.
Change to 4½mm (US 7) needles.
Row 5 (RS): Knit.
Row 6: K4, P to last 4 sts, K4.
Rep last 2 rows 14 times more, ending with a WS row.
Beg with a K row, cont in st st until back measures 46 (47: 47: 48: 48: 49)cm/18¼ (18½: 18½: 19: 19: 19½)in, ending with a WS row.
Shape armholes
Cast off 5 (6: 6: 7: 7: 8) sts at beg of next 2 rows. 91 (93: 99: 101: 107: 109) sts.
Dec 1 st at each end of next 5 (5: 7: 7: 9: 9) rows, then on foll 4 alt rows, then on every foll 4th row until 69 (71: 73: 75: 77: 79) sts rem.
Cont straight until armhole measures 23 (23:

24: 24: 25: 25)cm/9 (9: 9½: 9½: 9¾: 9¾)in, ending with a WS row.
Shape shoulders and back neck
Cast off 5 (5: 5: 6: 6: 6) sts at beg of next 2 rows. 59 (61: 63: 63: 65: 67) sts.
Next row (RS): Cast off 5 (5: 5: 6: 6: 6) sts, K until there are 9 (9: 10: 9: 9: 10) sts on right needle and turn, leaving rem sts on a holder. Work each side of neck separately.
Cast off 4 sts at beg of next row.
Cast off rem 5 (5: 6: 5: 5: 6) sts.
With RS facing, rejoin yarn to rem sts, cast off centre 31 (33: 33: 33: 35: 35) sts, K to end.
Complete to match first side, reversing shapings.

FRONT

Work as given for back until 8 (10: 10: 10: 10: 10) rows less have been worked than on back to start of shoulder shaping, ending with a WS row.
Shape neck
Next row (RS): K24 (25: 26: 27: 27: 28) and turn, leaving rem sts on a holder.
Work each side of neck separately.
Cast off 5 sts at beg of next row. 19 (20: 21: 22: 22: 23) sts.
Dec 1 st at neck edge of next 3 rows, then on foll 1 (2: 2: 2: 2: 2) alt rows. 15 (15: 16: 17: 17: 18) sts.
Work 1 row, ending with a WS row.
Shape shoulder
Cast off 5 (5: 5: 6: 6: 6) sts at beg of next and foll alt row.
Work 1 row.
Cast off rem 5 (5: 6: 5: 5: 6) sts.
With RS facing, rejoin yarn to rem sts, cast off centre 21 (21: 21: 21: 23: 23) sts, K to end.
Complete to match first side, reversing shapings.

SLEEVES (both alike)

Cast on 67 (69: 69: 71: 73: 73) sts using 4mm (US 6) needles.
Work in garter st for 4 rows, ending with a WS row.

Change to 4½mm (US 7) needles.
Beg with a K row, cont in st st, shaping sides by dec 1 st at each end of 9th and every foll 6th row to 59 (61: 61: 63: 65: 65) sts, then on every foll 8th row until 53 (55: 55: 57: 59: 59) sts rem.
Work 5 rows, ending with a WS row.
Inc 1 st at each end of next and every foll 4th row to 59 (61: 67: 67: 69: 75) sts, then on every foll 6th row until there are 69 (71: 73: 75: 77: 79) sts.
Cont straight until sleeve measures 44 (44: 44: 45: 45: 45)cm/17¼ (17¼: 17¼: 17¾: 17¾: 17¾)in, ending with a WS row.

Shape top
Cast off 5 (6: 6: 7: 7: 8) sts at beg of next 2 rows. 59 (59: 61: 61: 63: 63) sts.
Dec 1 st at each end of next 7 rows, then on foll 4 alt rows, then on every foll 4th row until 33 (33: 35: 35: 37: 37) sts rem.
Work 1 row, ending with a WS row.
Dec 1 st at each end of next and every foll alt row to 23 sts, then on foll 3 rows, ending with a WS row.
Cast off rem 17 sts.

MAKING UP
PRESS as described on page 123.
Join both shoulder seams using backstitch, or mattress stitch if preferred.

Collar
Cast on 98 (98: 98: 98: 114: 114) sts using 4mm (US 6) needles.
Row 1 (WS): K2, *P2, K2, rep from * to end.
Row 2: P2, *K2, P2, rep from * to end.
These 2 rows form rib.
Cont in rib until collar measures 8cm//3¼in, ending with a WS row.
Next row (RS): Rib 24 (24: 24: 24: 28: 28), M1, K1, place marker on needle, K1, M1, rib 46 (46: 46: 46: 54: 54), M1, K1, place marker on needle, K1, M1, rib to end. 102 (102: 102: 102: 118: 118) sts.
Next row: *Rib to within 1 st of marker, M1, P2 (marker is between these 2 sts), M1, rep

from * once more, rib to end.
Next row: *Rib to within 1 st of marker, M1, K2 (marker is between these 2 sts), M1, rep from * once more, rib to end.
Rep last 2 rows 12 times more. 206 (206: 206: 206: 222: 222) sts.
Cast off in rib.
Join row-end edges of collar. Matching sts directly below markers to centre front and back neck, sew cast-on edge of collar to neck edge.

Fringe edging
With RS facing and using 3.50mm (US E-4) crochet hook, rejoin yarn to cast-off edge of collar level with seam, 1ch (does NOT count as st), work 1 row of dc evenly around cast-off edge of collar, ending with 1ss in first dc.
Next round (RS): 1ch (does NOT count as st), (1dc, 16ch and 1dc) in each dc to end, 1ss in first dc.
Fasten off.
Join sleeve seams, then work fringe edging around lower edge of sleeves in same way.
See page 124 for finishing instructions, setting in sleeves using the set-in method and leaving side seams open for first 34 rows.

CABLE-RIB SWEATER

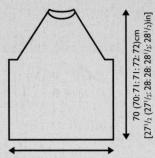

54 (56.5: 59.5: 62: 64.5: 67.5)cm
[21¼ (22¼: 23¼: 24¼: 25½: 26½)in]

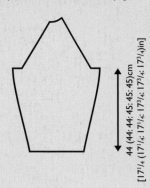

SIZES

1	2	3	4	5	6

TO FIT BUST

91	97	102	107	112	117	cm
36	38	40	42	44	46	in

YARN

Rowan Cotton Glace – dark plum (806)

19	19	20	21	21	22 x 50gm

NEEDLES

1 pair 2¾mm (no 12) (US 2) needles
1 pair 3¼mm (no 10) (US 3) needles
Cable needle

TENSION

30 sts and 36 rows to 10cm/4in measured over pattern using 3¼mm (US 3) needles.

SPECIAL ABBREVIATION

C3B = slip next 2 sts onto cable needle and leave at back of work, K1 tbl, slip the P st from cable needle back onto left needle and P this st, then K1 tbl from cable needle.

BACK

Cast on 162 (170: 178: 186: 194: 202) sts using 2¾mm (US 2) needles.
Row 1 (RS): K3 (0: 4: 1: 0: 2), (P1, K1 tbl) 0 (0: 0: 0: 2: 0) times, P0 (0: 0: 0: 1: 0), *K2, (P1, K1 tbl) twice, P1, rep from * to last 5 (2: 6: 3: 0: 4) sts, K5 (2: 6: 3: 0: 4).
Row 2: P3 (0: 4: 1: 0: 2), (K1, P1 tbl) 0 (0: 0: 0: 2: 0) times, K0 (0: 0: 0: 1: 0), *P2, (K1, P1 tbl) twice, K1, rep from * to last 5 (2: 6: 3: 0: 4) sts, P5 (2: 6: 3: 0: 4).
Row 3: K3 (0: 4: 1: 0: 2), (P1, C3B, P1) 0 (0: 0: 0: 1: 0) times, *K2, P1, C3B, P1, rep from * to last 5 (2: 6: 3: 0: 4) sts, K5 (2: 6: 3: 0: 4).
Row 4: As row 2.
These 4 rows form patt.
Cont in patt for a further 4 rows, ending with a WS row.
Change to 3¼mm (US 3) needles.
Cont in patt until back measures 43cm/17in, ending with a WS row.

Shape raglan armholes

Keeping patt correct, cast off 8 sts at beg of next 2 rows. 146 (154: 162: 170: 178: 186) sts.
Dec 1 st at each end of next 7 (11: 17: 23: 27: 33) rows, then on every foll alt row until 48 (50: 50: 50: 52: 52) sts rem.
Work 1 row, ending with a WS row.

Shape back neck

Next row (RS): Work 2 tog, patt 4 sts and turn, leaving rem sts on a holder.
Work each side of neck separately.
Dec 1 st at beg of next row.
Cast off rem 4 sts.
With RS facing, rejoin yarn to rem sts, cast off centre 36 (38: 38: 38: 40: 40) sts, patt to last 2 sts, work 2 tog.
Complete to match first side, reversing shapings.

FRONT

Work as given for back until 66 (70: 70: 70: 72: 72) sts rem in raglan armhole shaping.
Work 1 row, ending with a WS row.

Shape neck

Next row (RS): Work 2 tog, patt 22 (24: 24: 24: 24: 24) sts and turn, leaving rem sts on a holder.
Work each side of neck separately.
Cast off 5 sts at beg of next and foll alt row and at same time dec 1 st at raglan armhole edge on 2nd row. 12 (14: 14: 14: 14: 14) sts.
Dec 1 st at each end of next and every foll alt row until 2 sts rem.
Work 1 row, ending with a WS row.
Next row (RS): K2tog and fasten off.
With RS facing, rejoin yarn to rem sts, cast off centre 18 (18: 18: 18: 20: 20) sts, patt to last 2 sts, work 2 tog.
Complete to match first side, reversing shapings.

SLEEVES

Cast on 79 (81: 81: 83: 85: 85) sts using 2¾mm (US 2) needles.
Row 1 (RS): P0 (1: 1: 0: 1: 1), (K1 tbl, P1)

0 (0: 0: 1: 1: 1) times, *K2, (P1, K1 tbl) twice,
P1, rep from * to last 2 (3: 3: 4: 5: 5) sts, K2,
(P1, K1 tbl) 0 (0: 0: 1: 1: 1) times, P0 (1: 1: 0:
1: 1).

Row 2: K0 (1: 1: 0: 1: 1), (P1 tbl, K1) 0 (0: 0: 1:
1: 1) times, *P2, (K1, P1 tbl) twice, K1, rep
from * to last 2 (3: 3: 4: 5: 5) sts, P2, (K1, P1
tbl) 0 (0: 0: 1: 1: 1) times, K0 (1: 1: 0: 1: 1).

Row 3: P0 (1: 1: 0: 1: 1), (K1 tbl, P1) 0 (0: 0: 1:
1: 1) times, *K2, P1, C3B, P1, rep from * to last
2 (3: 3: 4: 5: 5) sts, K2, (P1, K1 tbl) 0 (0: 0: 1: 1:
1) times, P0 (1: 1: 0: 1: 1).

Row 4: As row 2.

These 4 rows form patt.

Cont in patt for a further 4 rows, inc 1 st
at each end of 3rd of these rows and
ending with a WS row. 81 (83: 83: 85: 87:
87) sts.

Change to 3¼mm (US 3) needles.

Cont in patt, shaping sides by inc 1 st at each
end of 3rd and every foll 4th row to 119 (121:
127: 125: 127: 133) sts, then on every foll 6th
row until there are 139 (141: 143: 145: 147:
149) sts, taking inc sts into patt.

Cont straight until sleeve measures 44 (44: 44:
45: 45: 45)cm/17¼ (17¼: 17¼: 17¾: 17¾:
17¾)in, ending with a WS row.

Shape raglan

Keeping patt correct, cast off 8 sts at beg of
next 2 rows. 123 (125: 127: 129: 131: 133) sts.

Dec 1 st at each end of next 13 rows, then on
every foll alt row until 23 sts rem.

Work 1 row, ending with a WS row.

Left sleeve only

Dec 1 st at each end of next row, then cast
off 4 sts at beg of foll row. 17 sts.

Dec 1 st at beg of next row, then cast off
5 sts at beg of foll row. 11 sts.

Rep last 2 rows once more.

Right sleeve only

Cast off 5 sts at beg and dec 1 st at end of
next row. 17 sts.

Work 1 row.

Rep last 2 rows twice more.

Both sleeves

Cast off rem 5 sts.

MAKING UP

PRESS as described on page 123.

Join both front and both back raglan seams
using backstitch, or mattress stitch if
preferred.

Collar

Cast on 172 (179: 179: 179: 186: 186) sts using
2¾mm (US 2) needles.

Row 1 (RS): K1 tbl, P1, K1 tbl, *(P1, K1 tbl)
twice, P1, K2, rep from * to last 8 sts, (P1, K1
tbl) 4 times.

Row 2: P1 tbl, K1, P1 tbl, *(K1, P1 tbl) twice,
K1, P2, rep from * to last 8 sts, (K1, P1 tbl) 4
times.

Row 3: K1 tbl, P1, K1 tbl, *P1, C3B, P1, K2,
rep from * to last 8 sts, P1, C3B, (P1, K1 tbl)
twice.

Row 4: As row 2.

These 4 rows form patt.

Cont in patt until collar measures 10cm/4in,
ending with a WS row.

Change to 3¼mm (US 3) needles.

Cont in patt until collar measures 19cm/7½in,
ending with a WS row.

Cast off 17 (18: 18: 18: 19: 19) sts at beg of
next 6 rows.

Cast off rem 70 (71: 71: 71: 72: 72) sts.

See page 124 for finishing instructions.

Overlap ends of collar by 3cm/1¼in and sew
cast-off edge to neck edge, positioning
overlapped section at centre front.

LACE-FRILL JACKET

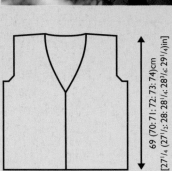

57.5 (60.5: 62.5: 66: 68: 71)cm
[22³/₄ (23³/₄: 24¹/₂: 26: 27: 28)in]

69 (70: 71: 72: 73: 74)cm
[27¹/₄ (27¹/₂: 28: 28¹/₄: 28³/₄: 29¹/₄)in]

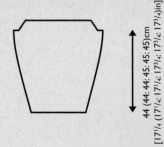

44 (44: 44: 45: 45: 45)cm
[17¹/₄ (17¹/₄: 17¹/₄: 17³/₄: 17³/₄: 17³/₄)in]

SIZES

1	2	3	4	5	6

TO FIT BUST

| 91 | 97 | 102 | 107 | 112 | 117 | cm |
| 36 | 38 | 40 | 42 | 44 | 46 | in |

YARNS

Jaeger Extra Fine Merino Aran
A burgundy (546)

15	16	17	18	19	20 x 50gm

Rowan Kidsilk Haze
B burgundy (595)

3	3	3	3	3	3 x 25gm

NEEDLES

1 pair 4mm (no 8) (US 6) needles
1 pair 4¹/₂mm (no 7) (US 7) needles
3³/₄mm (no 9) (US 5) circular needle

TENSION

19 sts and 25 rows to 10cm/4in measured over st st using 4¹/₂mm (US 7) needles and yarn A.

BACK

Cast on 109 (115: 119: 125: 129: 135) sts using 4mm (US 6) needles and yarn A.
Row 1 (RS): K2 (0: 1: 0: 0: 0), P3 (2: 3: 1: 3: 0), *K3, P3, rep from * to last 2 (5: 1: 4: 0: 3) sts, K2 (3: 1: 3: 0: 3), P0 (2: 0: 1: 0: 0).
Row 2: P2 (0: 1: 0: 0: 0), K3 (2: 3: 1: 3: 0), *P3, K3, rep from * to last 2 (5: 1: 4: 0: 3) sts, P2 (3: 1: 3: 0: 3), K0 (2: 0: 1: 0: 0).
These 2 rows form rib.
Cont in rib for a further 12 rows, ending with a WS row.
Change to 4¹/₂mm (US 7) needles.
Beg with a K row, cont in st st until back measures 46 (47: 47: 48: 48: 49)cm/18¹/₄ (18¹/₂: 18¹/₂: 19: 19: 19¹/₂)in, ending with a WS row.
Shape armholes
Cast off 3 sts at beg of next 2 rows. 103 (109: 113: 119: 123: 129) sts.
Dec 1 st at each end of next 6 rows. 91 (97: 101: 107: 111: 117) sts.

Cont straight until armhole measures 23 (23: 24: 24: 25: 25)cm/9 (9: 9¹/₂: 9¹/₂: 9³/₄: 9³/₄)in, ending with a WS row.
Shape shoulders and back neck
Cast off 10 (11: 11: 12: 13: 14) sts at beg of next 2 rows. 71 (75: 79: 83: 85: 89) sts.
Next row (RS): Cast off 10 (11: 11: 12: 13: 14) sts, K until there are 14 (14: 16: 17: 16: 17) sts on right needle and turn, leaving rem sts on a holder.
Work each side of neck separately.
Cast off 4 sts at beg of next row.
Cast off rem 10 (10: 12: 13: 12: 13) sts.
With RS facing, rejoin yarn to rem sts, cast off centre 23 (25: 25: 25: 27: 27) sts, K to end.
Complete to match first side, reversing shapings.

LEFT FRONT

Cast on 55 (58: 60: 63: 65: 68) sts using 4mm (US 6) needles and yarn A.
Row 1 (RS): K2 (0: 1: 0: 0: 0), P3 (2: 3: 1: 3: 0), *K3, P3, rep from * to last 2 sts, K2.
Row 2: P2, K3, *P3, K3, rep from * to last 2 (5: 1: 4: 0: 3) sts, P2 (3: 1: 3: 0: 3), K0 (2: 0: 1: 0: 0).
These 2 rows form rib.
Cont in rib for a further 12 rows, ending with a WS row.
Change to 4¹/₂mm (US 7) needles.
Beg with a K row, cont in st st until 18 rows less have been worked than on back to beg of armhole shaping, ending with a WS row.
Shape front slope
Dec 1 st at end of next and every foll 4th row until 50 (53: 55: 58: 60: 63) sts rem.
Work 1 row, ending with a WS row.
Shape armhole
Cast off 3 sts at beg of next row. 47 (50: 52: 55: 57: 60) sts.
Work 1 row.
Dec 1 st at armhole edge of next 6 rows **and at same time** dec 1 st at front slope edge on next and foll 4th row. 39 (42: 44: 47: 49: 52) sts.
Dec 1 st at front slope edge **only** on 3rd and

KNITTING TECHNIQUES

Included here is information that will help you follow knitting patterns and achieve success with your knits. (See page 124 for knitting abbreviations.)

TENSION

Obtaining the correct tension (the correct number of stitches and rows per cm/in) will ensure a successful piece of knitting. It is especially important for knitted garments, as tension controls both the shape and size of an article. It is recommended that you knit a square in the pattern stitch and/or stocking stitch of perhaps 5 to 10 more stitches and 5 to 10 more rows than those given in the tension note. Mark the central 10cm/4in square with pins and count the number or rows and stitches within this area. If you have more stitches and rows than the recommended tension, try again using thicker needles; if you have fewer stitches and rows, try again using finer needles.

Once you have achieved the correct tension, your garment will be knit to precisely the measurements indicated.

SIZES

In a pattern that is written for more than one size, the first figure in the set of figures for different sizes is for the smallest size and the figures for the larger sizes are inside the parentheses. When there is only one set of figures, this applies to all sizes. Be sure to follow the set of figures for your chosen size throughout. (Also, follow either the centimeter or inch measurements throughout.) If 0 (zero) or a – (hyphen) is given for your size, this instruction does not apply to your size.

When choosing which size to knit, measure one of your own garments that fits you comfortably.

Having chosen an appropriate pattern size based on width, look at the corresponding length for that size; if you are not happy with the recommended length, adjust your own garment before beginning your armhole shaping – any adjustment after this point will mean that the sleeve will not fit into your garment easily. Don't forget to take your adjustment into account if there is any side seam shaping.

Finally, look at the sleeve length, taking into account any top-arm insertion length. Measure your body between the centre of your neck and your wrist; this measurement should correspond to half the garment width plus the sleeve length. Again, your sleeve length may be adjusted, but remember to take into consideration your sleeve increases if you do adjust the length – you must increase more frequently than the pattern states to shorten your sleeve, less frequently to lengthen it.

CHART NOTE

Some of the patterns in this book are worked from charts. Each square on a chart represents a stitch and each line of squares a row of knitting. Each different yarn shade (or stitch instruction) used is given a colour or symbol, which is shown in the key with the chart. When working from the charts, read odd rows (knit) from right to left and even rows (purl) from left to right, unless otherwise stated.

FAIR ISLE COLOURWORK KNITTING

The Fair Isle technique is used when two or three colours are worked repeatedly across a row. To work this technique, strand the yarn not in use loosely across the wrong side of the knitting. If you are working with more than two colours, treat the floating yarns as if they were

one yarn and always spread the stitches to their correct width to keep them elastic. It is advisable not to carry the stranded or floating yarns over more than three stitches at a time, but to weave them under and over the colour you are working, catching them into the wrong side of the work.

FINISHING INSTRUCTIONS

The pieces for your knitted garment or other projects may take hours to complete, so it would be a great pity to spoil the work by taking too little care in the pressing and finishing process. Follow the following these tips for professional-looking knits.

PRESSING AND BLOCKING

Spread out each piece of knitting to the correct measurements and pin it to a backing cloth – this is called 'blocking'. Following the instructions on the yarn label, press the pieces, avoiding ribbing, garter-stitch areas and other raised textures such as cables. Take special care to press the edges, as this will make stitching seams both easier and neater. If the yarn label indicates that the fabric is not to be pressed, then cover the blocked out knitted fabric with a damp white cotton cloth and leave it to stand to create the desired effect. Darn in all ends neatly along the selvedge edge or a colour join, as appropriate.

STITCHING SEAMS

When stitching knitted pieces together, remember to match areas of colour and texture very carefully where they meet. Use a seam stitch such as backstitch or mattress stitch (an edge-to-edge stitch) for all main knitting seams. Join all ribbing (and neckbands) with mattress stitch, unless otherwise stated.

KNITTING ABBREVIATIONS

JOINING GARMENT PIECES

When stitching the seams on a knitted garment, start by joining the left shoulder and neckband seams as explained above. Then sew the top of the sleeve to the body of the garment using the method recommended in the pattern. The following are the techniques for different sleeve types.

Straight cast-off sleeves: Aligning the centre of the cast-off edge of the sleeve with the shoulder seam, sew the top of the sleeve to the body, using markers as guidelines where applicable.

Square set-in sleeves: Aligning the centre of the cast-off edge of the sleeve with the shoulder seam, set the sleevehead into the armhole so that the straight sides at the top of the sleeve form a neat right-angle with the armhole cast-off stitches on the back and front.

Shallow set-in sleeves: Aligning the centre of cast-off edge of sleeve with the shoulder seam, join the cast-off stitches at the beginning of the armhole shaping with the cast-off stitches at the start of the sleevehead shaping. Sew the sleevehead into the armhole, easing in the shapings.

Set-in sleeves: Aligning the centre of the cast-off edge of sleeve with the shoulder seam, set in the sleeve, easing the sleevehead into the armhole. After joining the top of the sleeves to the back and front of the garment, join the side and sleeve seams.

Next, slip stitch any pocket edgings and linings in place, and sew on buttons to correspond with buttonholes.

Lastly, press seams, avoiding ribbing and any areas of garter stitch.

The following abbreviations are used for the patterns in this book. Explanations for special abbreviations are given with the patterns.

alt	alternate
approx	approximately
beg	begin(ning)
cm	centimetre(s)
cont	continu(e)(ing)
dec	decreas(e)(ing)
foll(s)	follow(s)(ing)
g st	garter stitch (K every row)
in	inch(es)
inc	increas(e)(ing); in a row instruction work into front and back of stitch
K	knit
m	metre(s)
M1	make one stitch by picking up horizontal loop before next stitch and knitting into back of it
M1P	make one stitch by picking up horizontal loop before next stitch and purling into back of it
meas	measures
mm	millimetre(s)
oz	ounce(s)
P	purl
patt	pattern
psso	pass slipped stitch over
p2sso	pass 2 slipped stitches over
rem	remain(s)(ing)
rep	repeat(ing)
rev st st	reverse stocking stitch (P all RS rows, K all WS rows)
RS	right side(s)
sl 1	slip one stitch
sL1K	slip one knitwise
sL1P	slip one purlwise
st(s)	stitch(es)

st st	stocking stitch (K all RS rows, P all WS rows)
tbl	through back of loop(s)
tog	together
WS	wrong side(s)
yd	yard(s)
yfrn	yarn forward and round needle
yfwd	yarn forward
yon	yarn over right needle
yrn	yarn round needle

CROCHET TERMS

UK crochet terms and abbreviations have been for the crochet instructions in this book. The list below gives the US equivalent where they vary.

UK	US
chain (ch)	chain (ch)
slip stitch (ss)	slip stitch (slip st)
double crochet (dc)	single crochet (sc)
half treble (htr)	half double (hdc)
treble (tr)	double crochet (dc)
double treble (dtr)	treble (tr)
triple treble (trtr)	double treble (dtr)
quadruple treble (qtr)	triple treble (trtr)
skip	miss

YARN INFORMATION

The following list covers the Rowan and Jaeger yarns used in this book. All the information was correct at the time of publication, but yarn companies change their products frequently and cannot absolutely guarantee that the shades or yarn types used will be available when you come to use these patterns.

For the best results, always use the yarn specified in your knitting pattern. Contact the distributors on page 126 to find a stockist of Rowan yarn or Jaeger yarn near you. For countries not listed, contact the main office in the U.K.

The yarn descriptions here will help you find a substitute if necessary. When substituting yarn, always remember to calculate the yarn amount needed by ball length rather than by ball weight.

Note: Always check the yarn label for care instructions.

JAEGER EXTRA FINE MERINO ARAN

An Aran-weight wool yarn; 100 per cent merino wool; approx 87m/95yd per 50g/1¾oz ball; 19 sts and 25 rows to 10cm/4in measured over st st using 4½mm (US size 7) needles.

JAEGER EXTRA FINE MERINO CHUNKY

An chunky-weight wool yarn; 100 per cent merino wool; approx 63m/69yd per 50g/1¾oz ball; 15 sts and 20 rows to 10cm/4in measured over st st using 6mm (US size 10) needles.

JAEGER EXTRA FINE MERINO DK

An medium-weight wool yarn; 100 per cent extra fine merino wool; approx 125m/137yd per 50g/1¾oz ball; 22 sts and 30–32 rows to 10cm/4in measured over st st using 3¾–4mm (US sizes 3–6) needles.

ROWAN ALL SEASON COTTON

A medium-weight cotton-mix yarn; 60 per cent cotton, 40 per cent acrylic/microfibre; approx 90m/99yd per 50g/1¾oz ball; 16–18 sts and 23–25 rows to 10cm/4in measured over st st using 4½–5½mm (US sizes 7–9) needles.

ROWAN CALMER

A medium-weight cotton-mix yarn; 75 per cent cotton, 25 per cent acrylic/microfibre; approx 160m/175yd per 50g/1¾oz ball; 21 sts and 30 rows to 10cm/4in measured over st st using 5mm (US size 8) needles.

ROWAN COTTON GLACE

A lightweight cotton yarn; 100 per cent cotton; approx 115m/126yd per 50g/1¾oz ball; 23 sts and 32 rows to 10cm/4in measured over st st using 3¼–3¾mm (US sizes 3–5) needles.

ROWAN DENIM

A medium-weight cotton yarn; 100 per cent cotton; approx 93m/102yd per 50g/1¾oz ball; 20 sts and 28 rows (before washing) and 20 sts and 32 rows (after washing) to 10cm/4in measured over st st using 4mm (US size 6) needles.

ROWAN 4PLY COTTON

A lightweight cotton yarn; 100 per cent cotton; approx 170m/186yd per 50g/1¾oz ball; 27–29 sts and 37–39 rows to 10cm/4in measured over st st using 3–3¼mm (US sizes 2–3) needles.

ROWAN 4PLY SOFT

A lightweight wool yarn; 100 per cent merino wool; approx 175m/191yd per 50g/1¾oz ball; 28 sts and 36 rows to 10cm/4in measured over st st using 3¼mm (US size 3) needles.

ROWAN KID CLASSIC

A medium-weight mohair-mix yarn; 70 per cent lambswool, 26 per cent kid mohair, 4 per cent nylon; approx 140m/153yd per 50g/1¾oz ball; 18–19 sts and 23–25 rows to 10cm/4in measured over st st using 5–5½mm (US sizes 8–9) needles.

ROWAN KIDSILK HAZE

A lightweight mohair-mix yarn; 70 per cent super kid mohair, 30 per cent silk; approx 210m/229yd per 25g/1oz ball; 18–25 sts and 23–34 rows to 10cm/4in measured over st st using 3¼–5mm (US sizes 3–8) needles.

ROWAN PLAID

A chunky-weight wool-mix yarn; 42 per cent merino wool, 30 per cent acrylic fibre, 28 per cent superfine alpaca; approx 100m/109yd per 100g/3½oz ball; 11–12 sts and 14–16 rows to 10cm/4in measured over st st using 8mm (US size 11) needles

ROWAN AND JAEGER YARN ADDRESSES

U.K.
Rowan Yarns, Green Lane Mill, Holmfirth,
West Yorkshire HD9 2DX, England.
Tel: +44 (0) 1484 681 881.
Fax: +44 (0) 1484 687 920.
www.knitrowan.com

AUSTRALIA
Australian Country Spinners
314 Albert Street, Brunswick, Victoria 3056.
Tel: (03) 9380 3888.

BELGIUM
Pavan, Meerlaanstraat 73,
B9860 Balegem (Oosterzele).
Tel: (32) 9 221 8594.
E-mail: pavan@pandora.be

CANADA
Diamond Yarn, 9697 St Laurent, Montreal,
Quebec, H3L 2N1.
Tel: (514) 388 6188.
Diamond Yarn (Toronto), 155 Martin Ross,
Unit 3, Toronto, Ontario M3J 2L9.
Tel: (416) 736 6111.
www.diamondyarns.com
E-mail: diamond@diamondyarn.com

DENMARK
Designvaerkstedet, Boulevarden 9, Aalborg
9000. Tel: (45) 9812 0713. Fax: (45) 9813 0213.
Inger's, Volden 19, Aarhus 8000.
Tel: (45) 8619 4044.
Sommerfuglen, Vandkunsten 3,
Kobenhaven K 1467. Tel: (45) 3332 8290.
E-mail: mail@sommerfuglen.dk
www.sommerfuglen.dk
Uldstedet, Fiolstraede 13, Kobehavn K 1171.
Tel/Fax: (45) 3391 1771.

Uldstedet, Gl. Jernbanevej 7, Lyngby 2800.
Tel/Fax: (45) 4588 1088.
Garnhoekeren, Karen Olsdatterstraede 9,
Roskilde 4000. Tel/Fax: (45) 4637 2063.

FRANCE
Elle Tricot, 8 Rue du Coq,
67000 Strasbourg. Tel: (33) 3 88 23 03 13.
E-mail: elletricot@agat.net
elletricot@agat.net. www.elletricote.com

GERMANY
Wolle & Design
Wolfshovener Strasse 76, 52428
Julich-Stetternich. Tel: (49) 2461 54735.
www.wolleunddesign.de
E-mail: Info@wolleunddesign.de

HOLLAND
de Afstap
Oude Leliestraat 12, 1015 AW Amsterdam.
Tel: (31) 20 6231445.

HONG KONG
East Unity Co Ltd
Unit B2, 7/F Block B, Kailey Industrial Centre,
12 Fung Yip Street, Chai Wan.
Tel: (852) 2869 7110. Fax (852) 2537 6952.
E-mail: eastuni@netvigator.com

ICELAND
Storkurinn, Laugavegi 59, 101 Reykjavik.
Tel: (354) 551 8258. Fax: (354) 562 8252.
E-mail: malin@mmedia.is

JAPAN
Puppy Co Ltd, T151-0051, 3-16-5 Sendagaya,
Shibuyaku, Tokyo. Tel: (81) 3 3490 2827.
E-mail: info@rowan-jaeger.com

KOREA
De Win Co Ltd, Chongam Bldg, 101,
34-7 Samsung-dong, Seoul. Tel: (82) 2 511 1087.
E-mail: knittking@yahoo.co.kr www.dewin.co.kr
My Knit Studio, (3F) 121 Kwan Hoon Dong,
Chongro-ku, Seoul. Tel: (82) 2 722 0006.
E-mail : myknit@myknit.com

NEW ZEALAND
Alterknitives, PO Box 47961, Ponsonby,
Auckland. Tel: (64) 9 376 0337.
E-mail: knitit@ihug.co.nz
Knit World, PO Box 30 645, Lower Hutt.
Tel: (64) 4 586 4530.
E-mail: knitting@xtra.co.nz
The Stitchery, Shop 8,
Suncourt Shopping Centre, 1111 Taupo.
Tel: (64) 7 378 9195.

NORWAY
Paa Pinne, Tennisvn 3D, 0777 Oslo.
Tel: (47) 909 62 818. www.paapinne.no
E-mail: design@paapinne.no

SPAIN
Oyambre, Pau Claris 145, 80009 Barcelona. Tel:
(34) 670 011957.
E-mail : comercial@oyambreonline.com

SWEDEN
Wincent, Norrtullsgatan 65, 113 45 Stockholm.
Tel: (46) 8 33 70 60.
E-mail: wincent@chello.se www.wincent.nu

U.S.A.
Rowan USA, c/o Westminster Fibers Inc,
4 Townsend West, Suite 8, Nashua, NI 1 03063.
Tel: +1 (603) 886 5041/5043.
E-mail: rowan@westminsterfibers.com

ACKNOWLEDGEMENTS

Authors' acknowledgements

We would like to thank:
Kate Buller for giving us the opportunity to
create this book; the team at Rowan for their
great support; Sue Whiting and Stella Smith
for the hours spent writing and checking the
patterns; Susan Berry, Georgina Rhodes,
Peter Williams and the models for turning the
concept into a visual reality and Sally Harding for
her editing skills.

Martin Storey would also like to specially thank:
Mark, for his steadfast support, my mother
Margaret, my sister Linda, Aunty Bette and
Aunty Pix for their patience in teaching me the
joys of the craft of hand knitting.

Sharon Brant would also like to specially thank:
All the knitters: Mrs Oakes, Mary, Joy, Gilly, Betty,
Ruby, Heather, Elaine, Peggy, Dodie, Anna and
Eleanor for her crochet expertise. My mum,
Thelma, for all the hours and patience in finishing
the garments and for always being there.

Publishers' acknowledgements

We would like to thank: the models,
Marian Sharp, Jan Plackett, Molly Haskey,
Bluebell Martin, Poppy Martin, Kristy Jones
and Sally Turnbull for their enthusiasm and
sense of fun. Julia Griffiths for her generosity,
advice and location. Carol Greenfield and
Patricia Soper for taking care of hair and
make-up. Lenka Paskuova and Chloe Palmer
for being great assistants.